BLACKSMITHING

A Guide to Practical Metalworking, Tools, and Techniques

BLACKSMITHING
A Guide to Practical Metalworking, Tools, and Techniques

DANIEL JOHNSON

amber
BOOKS

First published in 2023

Published by
Amber Books Ltd
United House
North Road
London N7 9DP
United Kingdom
www.amberbooks.co.uk
Instagram: amberbooksltd
Facebook: amberbooks
Pinterest: amberbooksltd

Editor: Michael Spilling
Designer: Mark Batley
Picture researcher: Terry Forshaw

ISBN: 978-1-83886-313-5

Printed in China

DISCLAIMER
This book is for information purposes only and the reader should
undertake any practices described in these pages at their own risk.
The techniques described in this book are dangerous and should
be approached with the utmost caution and following the correct
safety procedures. Neither the author or the publisher can accept
responsibility for any loss, injury or damage caused as a result
of using the blacksmithing techniques described in this book,
nor for any prosecutions or proceedings brought or instigated
against any persons that may result from using these techniques.

CONTENTS

PROJECTS

WHAT IS BLACKSMITHING?

This book will discuss the basics of blacksmithing,
from the various techniques to the tools of the
trade. The terms 'blacksmithing' and 'blacksmith'
historically referred to the working of iron, which
when heated would form a black oxide.

ANCIENT CRAFT
A blacksmith is shown using a hammer and tongs on this
Attic red-figure terracotta drinking cup dating from the 6th
century BCE.

Alongside instructions in the basics of blacksmithing, there are several projects for the novice blacksmith to have a go at. The earlier projects teach the basic techniques and focus on achieving control.

While measurements are provided for each project, scrap metal can be used for all of them, to save costs. When using scrap, the measurements may not be as precise, but as long as they are fairly close to the ideal measurements there should be no issue. The projects can be scaled up or down so you can practise different aspects of forge work.

Blacksmithing Through the Ages

Blacksmiths were highly valued throughout history as they were relied upon to create tools of war, and also made and repaired everyday items for the entire community. Often situated in the heart of the village, they tended to repair iron cart tyres and everyday

COPPERSMITH
This 1st century AD marble relief from Pompei,
Italy, depicts a Roman coppersmith's shop in action.
Blacksmiths were respected craftsmen in the ancient
world, able to produce tools, utensils, household
items, weapons and armour.

tools. Blacksmiths were also needed at sea, where whenever possible a ship would carry a small forge for fixing items around the ship while underway.

As the 18th and 19th centuries saw the industrialization of crafts into mass-produced, affordable products, the number of blacksmiths inevitably declined. However, although the demand for new hand-made artifacts decreased, there was still a need for repairing many items, and blacksmiths found work in this area. As a result, a divide emerged between mass-produced items and hand-crafted pieces, leading to a more artisan-oriented approach in blacksmithing, as well as in other crafts.

Above: BUCOLIC SCENE
A blacksmith at work on an anvil outside his forge, c. 1857. In the early years of photography, such bucolic scenes capturing the lives of ordinary people, craftsmen, artisans and workers were popular.

Opposite: TRAVELLERS' FRIEND
***The Blacksmith's Shop* (oil on canvas, 1771), by Joseph Wright of Derby, England. Joseph Wright created five paintings on the theme of a blacksmith's shop or forge between the years 1771 and 1773. The scene shows a pair of blacksmiths forging a horseshoe so that a group of travellers can continue on their journey.**

The Basics

Blacksmithing may be daunting for beginners. The new blacksmith should take it slow to start with and learn the basics one step at a time. The techniques range in difficulty, with some better suited for learners, but as your skill grows, the items that can be made will become more complex and intricate as you gain in confidence and ability. As you learn more about the properties of other metals and materials and how to work them, experiment with shapes and forms.

Strength isn't the key to being a great blacksmith – tools like the power hammer have been invented to do the heavy work, so you can focus on the details. An alternative is to use lighter stock to make the work easier. Developing the ability to visualize the object you want to make in three dimensions from a sketch or drawing is also helpful. But at the end of the day, you just need to pick up a hammer and have a go; you will gain experience the more you forge.

Blacksmithing Today

Today, blacksmithing often involves making commissioned pieces, realizing your own or another's idea in three-dimensional metal form. It is a skill and a process that leaves a permanent imprint from the maker. There is a demand for the blacksmith in historical restoration, along with other heritage crafts, to restore and repair historical metalwork.

There is a difference between blacksmiths and farriers: a blacksmith is trained in working iron and in structural building, whereas a farrier works with horses and needs training in blacksmithing to shape the shoe properly. Both are trained in blacksmithing techniques, but specialize in different areas.

The few universities that teach blacksmithing around the world include Hereford College of Arts in the UK, with an Artistic Blacksmithing degree course (BA) available. In the USA, the Southern Illinois University runs several metalworking courses and a masters (MA) in blacksmithing. The University of Gothenburg in Sweden runs a Programme in Applied Arts and Design, Metal Art.

STUDENT AT WORK
A blacksmith student works on quite an advanced project
involving creating a leaf head for a gate or fence.

BASIC TECHNIQUES

In blacksmithing, various techniques are used
to forge the material in the desired way. Some of
the basic methods described in this book include:
drawing down/out, bending, upsetting, punching,
scrolling, twisting, controlled spreading of material,
fire welding and riveting. These techniques can
be used individually or in combination to create
complex forged sculptures or gates, for example.

DRAWING

Drawing down or out is the process of forging (hammering) the material with the hammer blows hitting from the top of the material and rotating by 90 degrees between each blow to create an even four-sided taper.

Hammering and rotating by 180 degrees will produce a two-sided taper.

The hammer blows in this technique transform the thickness of the material into length.

SETTING DOWN

Setting down involves isolating a section of material by placing it over the edge of an anvil and striking the material. The action of your hammer blows landing half-off the anvil edge and half-on will cause the material to sink over the anvil edge but itself retain a straight top edge, in effect creating a step on the underside of the material.

Blows landing half-off the anvil edge and half-on will cause the material to sink over the edge.

A step is created on the underside of the materials.

BENDING

By using the heat in a length of metal bar and either hammering the material over the horn or the edge of an anvil, a gentle bend can be made on the bar. Other methods of getting a more controlled bend include using either a bending jig or tongs, a vice or bending forks.

A blacksmith uses the horn of an anvil to bend a metal bar.

TWISTING

The act of twisting a hot metal bar can create a subtle or not-so-subtle forge detail within the length of the bar. The twist is affected by how many sides there are to the metal bar; the more sides the bar has, the finer the style of the twist.

Heat can also be used to control the tightness of the twist in different sections of the bar. This is because areas that contain the most heat will move more easily than ones that are cooler.

UPSETTING

This technique is the opposite of drawing out material. It involves using heat in an isolated area of the metal bar and forging the material back into itself, in effect thickening the material over the heated area.

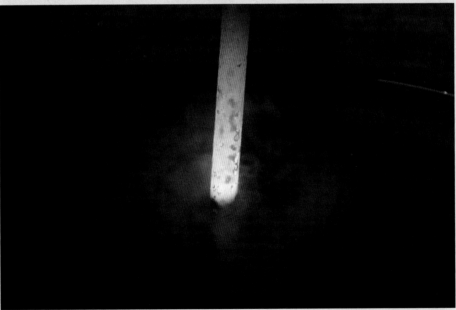

By quenching the end of a heated bar, you can create a sharp transition point, past which the material cannot easily be deformed.

The sharp termination of temperature within the bar can be seen clearly here.
The cooled steel will deform much less than the heated section.

UPSETTING (CONTINUED)

The finished result will be thicker than the starting stock. However, what you gain in thickness you lose in length.

Using a vessel, you can cool behind the tip and the area that you wish to upset in order to shorten the heat and create a more localized movement of material.

By placing the bar vertically on the anvil face and hitting the upright bar downwards, material in the heated section of the bar will swell, creating the upset.

PUNCHING

When forging, using a hot punch to put a hole through a metal bar is often the quickest method. This approach is faster than cooling the material and drilling it, as quenching can harden most forgeable metals to some degree.

First, mark the location of the hole on the cold piece of metal. Next, heat the material to a suitable temperature, then position a punch over the marked location.

Drilling through a material that has gained added hardness can take longer and cause drill bits to dull more quickly. As a result, the drilling process may take significantly longer than simply reheating the bar and using a hot punch to create the hole.

Hammer down on the punch to create a hole. Quench the punch to avoid it overheating.

SCROLLING

Scrolling is a blacksmithing technique in which a tapered bar is rolled up using the proportions of the golden spiral. This is a popular method for finishing off a bar. The process involves forging the material over the horn of the anvil, and then refining the shape of the scroll using bending dogs, a jig or scrolling tongs.

The tip of the bar is forged over the edge of the anvil to start the scroll.

Flip the bar 180 degrees so the scroll faces up and hammer it towards your body to refine the shape.
To achieve the necessary distance as the scroll opens up, flip the bar 180 degrees and hammer down to bend it.

The scroll can be tightened by hammering it in towards the body, as shown above.

POLISHING

Polishing is a crucial final step in finishing knives and other objects. It typically follows hand sanding up to around 400 grit and involves progressively smoothing the surface from rough to fine using similar techniques.

POLISHING MOPS
From bottom: a soft, unstitched cotton mop is often used for the final stage of polishing; a stitched cotton mop works as a medium-fine polishing tool; a stitched sisal mop is coarser and more durable that the other two types.

A general-purpose buffing compound can be applied to the mop using gentle pressure.
You should not apply too much compound; add more as you polish the item by hand.

Apply gentle pressure during rough polishing to effectively maintain machine speed and polish.

THE PRODUCTIVE WORKSHOP

A well laid-out workshop will benefit you in terms of both productivity and safety. Its layout should provide a logical flow around the workshop, with sufficient space between each machine and working area. Ideally, there should be a clear central area where you can draw full-size project layouts with chalk, if space permits.

IDEALLY, YOUR WORKSHOP should be situated with easy access for moving supplies and materials, as well as for getting your finished project out into the world once completed. A large roller shutter or garage door would be a good idea, with a separate door for people to enter and exit.

It is recommended that you make a list of all the equipment, machines, tools and so on that you will require in your workshop. Plan ahead and ensure you leave space for items that you cannot afford yet.

Create various layouts and consider them over a few days, then modify your plans if necessary until you have the best layout to maximize efficient workspace. Don't commit too strongly to any one layout until you know how it works on a practical level, and be prepared to alter your layout when you begin using your workshop. Flexibility is important.

THE IMPORTANCE OF APPROPRIATE VENTILATION

While working in a blacksmith workshop, it is essential to be aware of the potential risk of fumes. The most common fumes encountered are carbon monoxide and carbon dioxide, which are both odourless and colourless gases that are produced when fuels are burned to power forges.

If these gases are allowed to accumulate, you may begin to experience the effects of poisoning. In such cases, it is vital to exit the workshop immediately and seek fresh air. Additionally, opening windows and doors will help the workshop to ventilate. It is crucial to have proper ventilation in the workshop, allowing for free air flow and the replacement of gases with fresh air.

Solid fuel forges should also be fitted with a hood with a flue that vents all smoke and gases from the forge to the outside. Gas forges and welding fumes should also be dealt with adequately, using extraction to replenish the air. It is strongly advised that you research the correct safety procedures for each tool in the workshop during training.

How To Spot Fume Hazards

Recognizing potential hazards and avoiding dangerous situations is crucial when working in a workshop where various fumes are produced. There follows a list of metals that you should be mindful of due to their potentially hazardous fume emissions.

EQUIPMENT

Here is a suggested list of equipment that you may need in your workshop:

Forge – this could be gas, coal or induction powered

Lathe

Anvil

Power hammer

Bandsaw or power hacksaw (also known as a donkey saw)

Benches (fixed and mobile)

Pedestal drill

Milling machine

Grinding wheels

Guillotine

Compressor

Punches, presses etc

Zinc

Zinc is a metal that has a low melting point and a boiling point of 900°C (1,652°F). Above this point, it burns and forms zinc oxide smoke, which is associated with metal fume fever. Symptoms of metal fume fever can include fever, chills, coughing, fatigue, muscle aches and shortness of breath.

When working with metals that contain zinc and involve hot work, it's crucial to have proper ventilation. Below is a list of metals containing zinc and information on how to handle them safely. A good way to spot the presence of zinc burning is a bright green flame accompanied by billowing white smoke.

Brass

Brass, an alloy of copper and zinc, typically contains only about 10 per cent zinc. However, when brass is melted, the zinc can reach its boiling point and release hazardous fumes. To avoid this risk, it's important to work in a well-ventilated area when melting brass for casting. As long as the brass is not melted, the risk of zinc oxide formation is minimal.

Bronze

Bronze can contain varying amounts of zinc. When working with bronze, it is important to focus on temperature control to avoid burning the material and releasing harmful fumes. The most commonly used alloy for forging is silicon bronze, which contains some zinc. During forging, proper ventilation should be in place to deal with smoke.

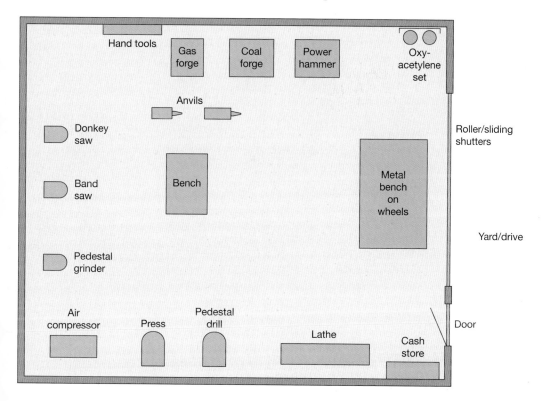

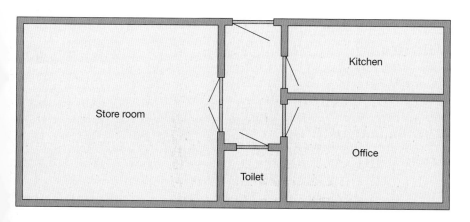

WORKSHOP LAYOUT
Designing a workshop layout is a personal process that depends on the given space and individual needs. The layout should prioritize ease of movement and functionality. The drawing shown here can serve as a guide or inspiration for your own workshop.

HEALTH AND SAFETY IN THE WORKSHOP

Always be sure to check local by-laws, health and safety guidelines, and regulatory requirements. Remember that you'll be creating noise, smoke and fumes, and you will be responsible for managing these correctly.

Your forge(s) will require canopies and ducting to take away smoke, fumes, dust and other particles, as will your welding bay and grinding areas. The floor of the workshop should be smooth and strong, able to withstand the forces produced by a power hammer, for example, and offering a safe, non-slip surface to walk on as you navigate your workshop.

Once you have decided on the layout of your workshop, you will need to make sure you have an adequate power supply and power outlets positioned correctly for each machine – a three-phase supply will probably be needed for at least some of your machines. Adequate lighting will also be needed, with extra lighting positioned by some machines to ensure your projects are well-lit and safe to work on. Be wary of fluorescent lighting, which can give a strobe effect on tools with moving parts, such as lathes. Forging areas require a lower lighting

level so you can observe the colour, and therefore temperature, of hot metal as you forge it.

You will need a steel rack located close by – outside the workshop is best – as well as a secure cage outside the workshop for holding gas bottles. A separate office space with a desk, drawing board and rest area (including a toilet if possible) is useful, along with a telephone and a computer with internet access. You'll also require a secure storeroom with adequate and strong shelving.

A clearly labelled COSHH (Control of Substances Hazardous to Health) cupboard for the safe storage of any hazardous chemicals – including anything from chemicals and dusts, to products like bleach, solvents and paint – is essential. An up-to-date list of its contents, along with all technical data sheets for each item, should be kept within easy access in the event of an emergency. You should also complete risk assessments (templates for which can be found online) and review these annually in keeping with your data sheets.

An adequate number of the correct fire extinguishers

should be located in the workshop for each type of fire (oil, electric, coal and so on), along with a fire blanket. There should also be a well stocked first aid box and a qualified first-aider on site.

Your workshop should include signs to show the locations of any emergency exits, as well as details on what to do in the event of a fire or accident, and a specifically designated and well-signed location in which to assemble in the event of a fire.

**COSHH CUPBOARD
A COSHH cupboard is an essential part of the workshop set-up.**

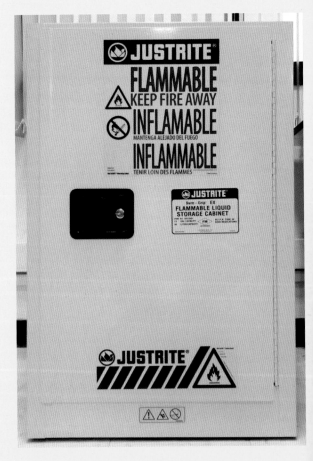

EAR DEFENDERS
Since blacksmithing is by its nature noisy, ear defenders should be used to preserve your hearing.

LEATHER GLOVES
These gloves offer an additional layer of protection, but prolonged contact with a hot bar can cause the heat to radiate into the glove. It is not recommended that you wear a glove on your hammer hand as the hammer may slip out.

SAFETY GLASSES

Proper eye protection is essential in the workshop and must be worn to safeguard your eyes against various potential hazards, such as sparks and wires from a wire wheel.

LEATHER APRON

A leather apron is a useful item to wear during both fire and general welding, as the leather material can prevent beads of molten metal from making contact with your clothing and skin.

OXY/PROPANE

A gas torch is a tool that combines compressed oxygen and propane through a nozzle to create a flame that can reach temperatures of up to 2,822°C (5,112°F). This makes it ideal for accurately heating small areas. The flame can be controlled by adjusting the flow and pressure of the fuel and oxidizer, allowing for a gentle reducing flame or a harsh oxidizing flame that can cut metal.

Galvanized/Galvannealed Steel

Galvanized steel is a type of steel that has a layer of zinc applied to its surface in order to prevent rusting. The most common method for applying this protective coating is by hot-dip galvanizing, which involves submerging the steel in a bath of molten zinc. Galvannealed steel is created by heating the zinc-coated steel to alloy the zinc and iron together, creating a stronger bond.

Galvanization is often used as a finish for ironwork that will be kept outside, but the process of cleaning up the finish can create zinc dust, which is hazardous if inhaled. Therefore, it is important to use a respirator when dealing with fettling (cleaning up rough edges on metalwork). It is crucial to note that galvanized steel should never be used in a forge, as it can produce large quantities of zinc oxide fumes that can quickly accumulate and cause harm.

Check the Alloy Before Use

Zinc isn't the only metal that can produce toxic or harmful fumes when heated or melted. Many steel alloys contain elements such as vanadium, silicon, nickel, manganese, chromium and copper, which can also release dangerous fumes. Therefore, it's crucial to research the alloy of

VENTILATION

Any blacksmithing workspace should be clearly ventilated before any work commences.

metal you wish to forge before heating it in the fire by chcking the composition of the metal when ordering your stock.

Grinding Abrasives and Polishing Compounds

When using abrasives or polishing compounds, appropriate personal protective equipment (PPE) must be used as the fumes and particulates from the abrasive and the material being cut are hazardous. Grinding, cutting and polishing should be done in areas with good ventilation or an extraction unit to replenish and filter the air.

A Tidy Workshop

Maintaining a clean and clutter-free workshop is essential for ensuring a safe working environment. When sweeping up metal dust and other types of debris, it is recommended that you wear a respirator to prevent you from inhaling hazardous particles.

LIGHTING

Having the right lighting in your workshop is important for safety and productivity. In the forge area, it's important to have enough lighting to see the heat of the material clearly to avoid over-heating and causing it to burn away. However, the brighter the lighting, the more washed-out the colour of the material appears. In areas where marking out or fine work is being done, a brighter lighting set-up can be used so you are not straining to see and can work safely.

MILLING MACHINE
A milling machine is not a necessary tool for blacksmithing, but it can be highly beneficial when used in conjunction with a lathe. This combination of tools makes it easier to create various tooling, provided that the operator has experience using them.

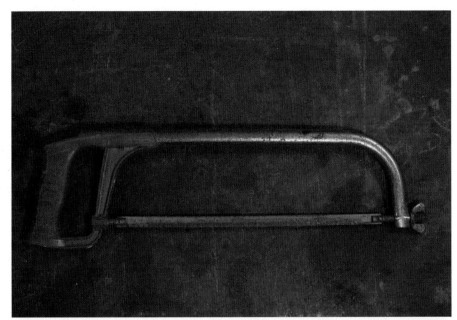

HACKSAW

The blade of a hacksaw consists of small, sharp teeth that only cut in one direction. Therefore, only light pressure is needed when moving in the cutting direction; too much can cause the blade to break or become stuck. No pressure at all should be applied when moving in the opposite direction.

Left: GUILLOTINE
A guillotine is used for cutting sheet metal in straight lines. However, curves can be achieved by removing excess material and gradually trimming closer to your scribed line, then filing.

Below: LATHE
Used to turn down bar stock to create parts or tools, a lathe is a handy tool when you are experienced with it. Care is required around a lathe to avoid getting caught and drawn into the machine.

PILLAR DRILL

The pillar drill is one of the most commonly used tools in a workshop, as it has the capability to drill holes up to 24mm (1in), depending on the job at hand. It is important to set the drill to the appropriate speed for the drill bit size and material being drilled before starting the process. This crucial information can usually be found online or may come with the drill bits.

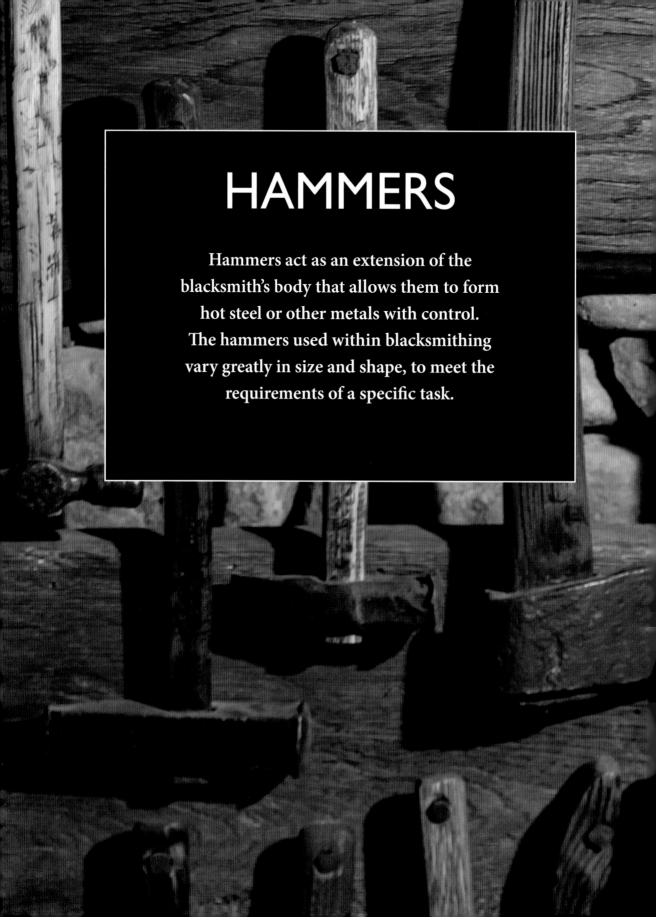

HAMMERS

Hammers act as an extension of the blacksmith's body that allows them to form hot steel or other metals with control. The hammers used within blacksmithing vary greatly in size and shape, to meet the requirements of a specific task.

IT IS IMPORTANT for blacksmiths to have a variety of hammers on hand to ensure they can complete any task safely and efficiently. What's more, using the wrong type of hammer could cause damage or leave an unwanted texture on the workpiece. When selecting a hammer for forging, you should consider its weight. Generally, one weighing 900–1,130g (2–2.5lb) is recommended as heavier hammers can cause muscle strains if used for extended periods of time.

MAINTAINING A RELIABLE HAMMER

Maintaining tools is essential for their longevity and performance. Over time, hammers may develop dents or chips on their faces, which can transfer that texture on to your workpiece. It's important to inspect your hammer regularly for any chips or cracks that may compromise its integrity. If you notice a chip, you can usually address it by grinding or filing it out. However, if you detect a crack, do not use the hammer for forging, as it may shatter under the force of striking and cause serious injury. Below are some steps you can take to keep your hammer in good shape:

Keep it clean: After each use, remove any debris or rust from the hammer using a wire brush. Wipe it down with a clean, dry cloth.

Lubricate the handle: Over time, the handle of the hammer can become dry and brittle, especially in a forge environment. To prevent

A blacksmith dishing steel using the ball peen of the hammer to push the material down into the hollow of the pipe. For this technique to be effective, the material must be either hot or annealed to prevent cracking.

Hammer Types

Listed below are some of the most common types of hammer used in blacksmithing:

Cross peen hammer: This hammer has a wedge-shaped head with one end rounded and the other end flat. It is used for controlling metal movement and creating texture.

Ball peen hammer: This hammer has a rounded head, with one end flat and the other end rounded. It is used for shaping and flattening metal, as well as for riveting.

Rounding hammer: This hammer has a round head and is used for moving more material during forging. It can also be used in areas where a curved face is needed, to lessen the chance of leaving marks in the steel.

Straight peen hammer: This hammer has a straight, flat head with one end rounded and the other end flat. The round end is used for forging in the same way as other hammers but the straight peen allows for clean, straight lines to be forged into the steel.

Chasing hammer: This has a long, narrow head with a rounded end. It is used for detailed work such as chasing and repoussé.

Sledgehammer: This hammer is used for shaping and flattening large stock-size steel with the help of another blacksmith working in tandem as smith and striker.

Hide and copper mallet: Hide and copper mallets are used to shape metal without leaving marks – especially for softer materials, such as brass and copper.

Power hammer: Although not a handheld tool, a power hammer is a mechanical hammer that exerts forces beyond those of a hand hammer. It is typically used for large-scale forging and can produce consistent results quickly.

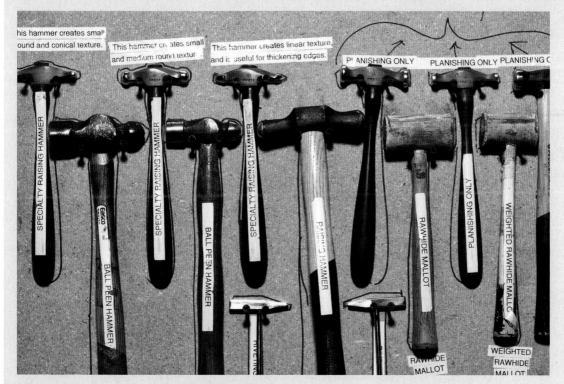

A range of hammers that can be used by metalworkers.

BALL PEEN HAMMER
A 900g (2lb) ball peen
hammer is often used for
general forging and dishing
of material.

this, occasionally apply a light coating of linseed or mineral oil to the handle, leave it overnight, then wipe excess away.

Check the wedges: The wedges that hold the head of the hammer to the handle can become loose over time. Check them periodically and tap them back into place if needed. Keeping the handle oiled will reduce the risk of the wedges coming loose.

Repolish the face: The face of the hammer can become worn or dented, affecting its ability to forge metal. Use a bench grinder or file to shape and then polish the face as needed.

Storage: When the hammer is not being used, it is important to store it in a dry and cool location, without exposing it to moisture or direct sunlight.

CHOOSING A FORGING HAMMER
Blacksmithing forging hammers come in many different weights and lengths depending on the work being done and the smith holding the hammer. However, a typical forging hammer is usually around 680–1,135g (1.5–2.5lb) with most blacksmiths choosing to use a 900g (2lb) hammer. While heavier hammers can be used for forging, they are typically best suited for heavier work that is less precise. A 900g (2lb) hammer is well-suited for moving material and some detail work, while lighter hammers excel in intricate detail work.

The length of hammer handles can range from 30.5 to 46cm (12–18in), with longer handles allowing for harder hits but less control. To quickly and easily find a suitable hammer handle length, measure from your palm to the top of your forearm. It's also important to

CROSS PEEN HAMMER
A 900g (2lb) cross peen hammer is mainly used in blacksmithing for directional forging, using the cross peen to spread material.

consider handle thickness as a handle that is too thick may be hard to grip, which can lead to less control and potential injury, while a handle that is too thin may not withstand the force of forging.

Overall, the weight and length of a blacksmith's forging hammer should be chosen based on the individual blacksmith's comfort, the type of work being done, and the amount of force needed to accomplish the task. Regular maintenance, such as keeping the hammer oiled and the face polished, will help to prolong its lifespan and ensure optimal performance.

USING A HIDE MALLET AND A COPPER MALLET

A hide mallet, also known as a rawhide mallet, is a tool used in blacksmithing to shape metal without marring or damaging the surface. Hide mallets come in different sizes, and the weight can range from a few ounces to several pounds. They are commonly used for shaping sheet metal, working with non-ferrous metals, and for delicate work on forged pieces.

Copper mallets are another common tool in blacksmithing. The head of the hammer is typically slightly rounded or flat, and it is used to strike metal without leaving marks or damaging the surface. Copper mallets are often used in conjunction with a chisel or punch for chasing, repoussé work and delicate shaping.

PLANISHING
Planishing is a metalworking technique that involves hammering a metal surface, typically copper, to smooth and polish it.

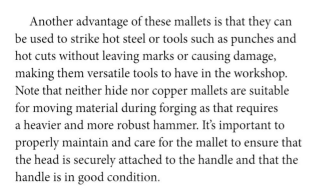

Another advantage of these mallets is that they can be used to strike hot steel or tools such as punches and hot cuts without leaving marks or causing damage, making them versatile tools to have in the workshop. Note that neither hide nor copper mallets are suitable for moving material during forging as that requires a heavier and more robust hammer. It's important to properly maintain and care for the mallet to ensure that the head is securely attached to the handle and that the handle is in good condition.

USING SLEDGEHAMMERS
In blacksmithing, a smith and striker are two individuals who work in unison to forge a piece of metal. The smith is the leader who controls the workpiece and uses tools such as fullers and swages to shape it, while the striker uses a heavy sledgehammer

FRENCH-STYLE HAMMER
These can be distinguished by the set-down top edge of the cross peen hammer. Functionally, there is no significant difference between the French-style cross peen and other types of cross peen hammers.

to deliver powerful blows to the workpiece on behalf of the smith. The use of a striker allows the smith to focus on controlling the metal while the striker provides the necessary force for shaping it, giving both power and delicate control during forging.

The purpose of using a smith and striker is to increase the efficiency and speed of the forging process. With the help of a striker, the smith can deliver more powerful blows to the metal and shape it more quickly than they would be able to do alone. Additionally, the use of a striker allows the smith to work on

Left:
CROSS PEEN HAMMER
Modern cross peens typically feature a manufacturing line along the side – a result of the drop hammer forging process used in their production.

Opposite:
SWEDISH-STYLE HAMMER
A blacksmith using a Swedish-style cross peen hammer. Although there's no functional difference compared to other styles of cross peen hammer, it is characterized by the swell at the centre of the hammer where the handle attaches.

Opposite: MALLETS
A selection of wooden, copper and leather mallets of various weights and sizes stored ready for use on a rack.

larger or more complex pieces of metal that would be too difficult for oneperson to handle alone. As a blacksmith, there are many occasions where having an extra pair of hands is essential.

Using a striker also helps to reduce fatigue and prevent injury. Blacksmithing is physically demanding work, and the repetitive motion of swinging a hammer can be tiring. By having a striker deliver the heavy blows, the smith can conserve their energy and prevent

Left: COPPER & HIDE MALLET
A combination copper and hide mallet offers the best of both worlds, providing the versatility of both mallets in a single tool.

Left: LEATHER MALLET
A leather mallet is much lighter than the combined copper version and therefore allows for lighter hits and ease of use.

NYLON & HIDE MALLET
The nylon side of this dual mallet can be used on cold metal to apply more force than a leather mallet.

900G (2LB) FORGING HAMMER
A 900g (2lb) forging hammer can be in any style as long as it has a flat forging face.

exhaustion or injury; while the smith reheats the metal and prepares for the next stage in forging, the striker gets to have a breather and recover. The use of a striker also allows the smith to maintain better control over the workpiece, reducing the risk of accidents or mistakes.

In traditional blacksmithing, the role of the striker is typically filled by an apprentice or assistant, who is trained to deliver powerful and accurate blows to the workpiece. However, in modern blacksmithing, the use of power hammers and other mechanical tools has made the role of the striker less common. Nonetheless, the technique of using a smith and a striker remains an important part of traditional blacksmithing and is still used by many skilled practitioners today.

AVOIDING INJURY
As with any physical activity, stretching is important for preparing the body for work and helping to prevent injury. Here are some stretches that can help avoid injury during work:

Neck stretch: Gently tilt your head to one side and hold for 10 seconds, then repeat on the other side.

Shoulder stretch: Place one hand on your opposite shoulder and gently pull your elbow across your chest, holding for 10 seconds. Repeat on the other side.

Chest stretch: Clasp your hands behind your back and straighten your arms, squeezing your shoulder blades together as much as possible.

Forearm stretch: Hold your arm out straight in front of you with your palm facing down, then gently pull your fingers back towards your wrist using your other hand, until you feel a stretch in your forearm.

Wrist stretch: Hold your arm out straight in front of you with your palm facing up, then use your other hand to gently press your fingers down towards your wrist, until you feel a stretch in your wrist.

Hip stretch: Stand with your feet shoulder-width apart and place your hands on your hips, then gently shift your weight from side to side, stretching your hips.

Hamstring stretch: Sit on the ground with your legs straight out in front of you, then lean forwards and reach towards your toes until you feel a stretch in your hamstrings. Hold for 10 seconds.

It's important to remember to warm up before stretching and to not overdo it. Stretching should be done gently and gradually, without any sudden or jerky movements. If you experience any pain or discomfort during stretching, or indeed during blacksmithing, stop and consult with a medical professional.

HOT CUT TOOL
A wooden handle on a hot cut tool reduces vibration and is easy and inexpensive to replace.

Right & opposite:
SMITH & STRIKER
A smith and striker working together to forge a taper. They start with heavy hammer blows from the striker and finish with the smith directing the striker with the use of the flatter tool to achieve a smooth surface.

Overleaf: FIRE WELDING
A smith and two strikers can use fire welding, an advanced blacksmithing technique that fuses iron or steel bars together. To ensure a strong weld, the bars must first be upset to increase their thickness and then have a step down forged into them, providing better grip and a greater surface area for fusion. The bars are then heated to near-molten temperatures without burning the metal and placed together to be hammered gently, setting the initial weld. After a few more heating rounds, the weld is consolidated. Note that a significant amount of material may oxidize during the heating process.

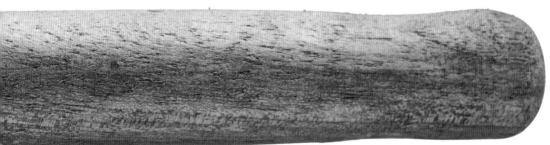

Above: SLEDGEHAMMER
This type of hammer is commonly used to shape and flatten stock-size pieces of steel, often with the help of another blacksmith acting as a striker.

Left & below:
RHYTHMIC HAMMER BLOWS
The use of rhythmic hammer blows in
blacksmithing can help to conserve stamina
and establish good pacing during work; often,
when turning the bar or taking a brief pause,
the hammer can be tapped on the anvil to
maintain energy and tempo.

Opposite: USING TWO HAMMERS
The combination of a smith and striker is
advantageous as it allows for the delivery of
directed, heavy hammer blows, enabling more
material to be moved in a heat as compared to
one smith.

Overleaf: BLACKSMITH AT WORK
A female blacksmith using isolated heat to
forge the front taper point of a fire poker.

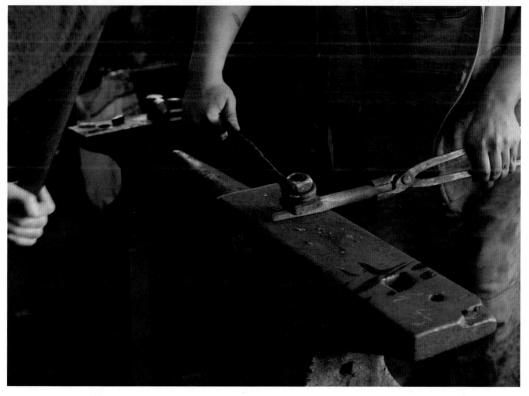

TONGS & VICES

When blacksmithing, there are many ways to hold
your work as you shape it with a hammer and
other tools. The method for holding your work
depends on the size and shape of the workpiece,
as well as the techniques being used.

THE PRITCHEL HOLE on the anvil is not just used for punching holes or straightening metal; it can also be used in combination with another tool called a holdfast. The holdfast is used to hold work on the anvil face, leaving the blacksmith with both hands free to use a hot cut tool, punch or drift to cut material or punch a hole. Having both hands available means that you can safely do the work without worrying about controlling a hot piece of metal.

VICES

One of the most fundamental tools to have in any workshop is a good, solid, metal bench vice. These are often cast steel and bolted to a workbench. They come in a range of sizes, from very small table-top vices to a blacksmith's leg vice. They are valuable in the fact that they can hold whatever is placed in the jaws very tightly, allowing for steel to be bent using one or to hold a workpiece while further work is done to it, such as heating with oxy/propane or riveting.

The main difference between a bench vice and a leg vice is that the cast body of the bench vice is not designed to handle heavy impacts, while the forged body of the leg vice, along with the leg that extends the vice to the floor, provides excellent support for heavy forging. This means that a leg vice is better suited than a bench vice for holding and shaping larger, heavier pieces of metal.

In conclusion, a vice is a valuable tool that provides a stable anchor for various processes, such as filing, cutting, drilling, bending, twisting, riveting and many others.

All photographs: HEAVY VICE
A heavy engineer's vice bolted to a moveable metalwork bench. While this cannot be hammered down upon like with a leg vice, the combination with the metalworkbench allows for mobility. The vice can be used to hold work while grinding, marking out or drilling. Make sure to have as much surface contact as possible with the object and the jaws of the vice to ensure the work is held safely and securely while it is being worked on.

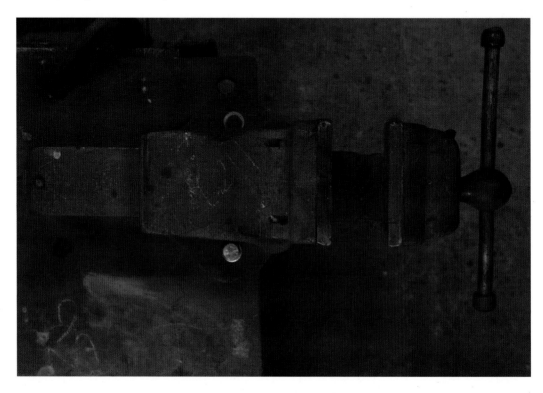

STAKES AND PITCH BOWL

The use of raising stakes in repoussé and chasing work allows for the creation of complex curved, raised or anticlastic shapes. The stakes are often forged from a thick bar of steel with a polished face of the desired shape at the top, which is used as an anvil to shape sheet metal.

Another method of holding sheet or repoussé work in place is through the use of pitch. Pitch is a mixture of tree sap and powders, such as charcoal, that can be adjusted to change its properties and make it harder or softer. After heating the pitch and pressing the workpiece into it to set, the piece can be hammered and engraved without slipping. Additionally, the pitch provides resistance to hammering on the presented side of the metal sheet, allowing for fine detail in repoussé work.

TONGS

Tongs are a fundamental tool in blacksmithing and are often custom-forged by the blacksmith to hold a specific size of stock. They come in various shapes and sizes, with long handles to provide a comfortable grip away from the heat of the forge and the workpiece. Tongs can be adjusted with heat and hammer blows to accommodate different sizes of stock.

Blacksmiths use a specific terminology to refer to the different types of tongs. Here are some common terms to help understand the naming of the tongs used:

Rivet tongs

Square bolt tongs

Opposite:
SCROLLING TONGS FOR FINE WORK
Due to having a forged pointed tip they can be used to fit into small areas to help move a bend to where you need it, allowing for careful adjustments to your work.

Bit or jaw – The part of the tongs that holds the workpiece is called the bit or jaw. It can be flat, round or V-shaped, depending on the shape of the stock.

Wolf jaw tongs: These tongs have jaws that are designed to grip round or square stock. This is a versatile jaw type and a kind of all-rounder, but not as effective as a dedicated set of tongs that are specifically designed for a particular type of stock.

Bolt tongs: These tongs have a curved jaw that allows them to grip stock that would not be easily held by standard tongs. The curve of the jaws allows for a different angle of hold and greater flexibility when gripping objects.

Flat jaw tongs: These tongs have flat jaws that are designed to hold flat stock, such as sheet metal or plate, or flat bar.

Hollow bit tongs/V-bit tongs: The jaws of these tongs are shaped like a half-circle or a V and have a groove that allows them to grip round or square stock with ease and reliability.

Scrolling tongs: These tongs have jaws that are shaped like long nose round pliers. They are commonly used for adjusting fine bends in metal scrollwork, giving it the final touch.

Faceplate or boss – The thick area where the reins meet the jaws on a set of tongs is called the faceplate or boss. This is the part of the tongs where the jaws are fixed or riveted together, providing stability and strength when gripping objects.

Reins or handles – The handles of the tongs are called reins.

A pair of flat-bit tongs.

Above: FIXING LINKS

Here, smaller scrolling tongs – otherwise known as round nose pliers or in this case, flat nose pliers – are being used to close the jump rings to make this chainmail.

Overleaf: TONGS AROUND THE FORGE

Blacksmiths often have a large collection of tongs in different shapes and sizes to accommodate a variety of workpieces. The ability to select the right pair of tongs for the job is an essential skill for any blacksmith.

All photographs: HANDLING TONGS WHEN QUENCHING
When performing the quench of a blade or tool it is important to avoid spilling the oil and to wear the correct PPE. The oil must be preheated to achieve a good quench. While quenching, the object must be fully submerged, to avoid igniting the smoke and fumes of the vaporizing oil. Keep your hands angled back away from the opening to avoid burning yourself.

ANVILS & ANVIL TOOLS

The anvil is synonymous with blacksmithing and one of the key tools, without which a blacksmith cannot function. It is the base upon which all products are forged. A vast range of tools are designed to be used with an anvil. The basics are described in this chapter.

THE ANVIL has many uses as a tool and can be broken down by its working faces and elements:

Horn: This is used for forging bends or drawing material down quickly.

Table: This is often used for hot cut work as it tends to be made of softer steel. Placing scrap metal under the bar being cut helps to further reduce damage to tools.

Face: This is where most of the forging work happens. It is typically tempered and hardened to resist the forging work.

Hardie hole: This square hole is used for holding the tools listed below.

Pritchel hole: This can be used in combination with a holdfast to hold work on the anvil face. It is also often used to punch through a material.

Anvils vary in size, shape and type of steel. The oldest may be made from wrought iron, which are soft compared to modern anvils. Being softer makes for less rebound when forging and more effort is needed to forge steel. The other downside is that due to being made from a softer metal they often sag in the centre, causing a dip in the face. This can cause your work to bend when it's being forged. More modern anvils are made of cast steel. These are a great option as they are normally in much better condition overall and will give a finer finish on your work.

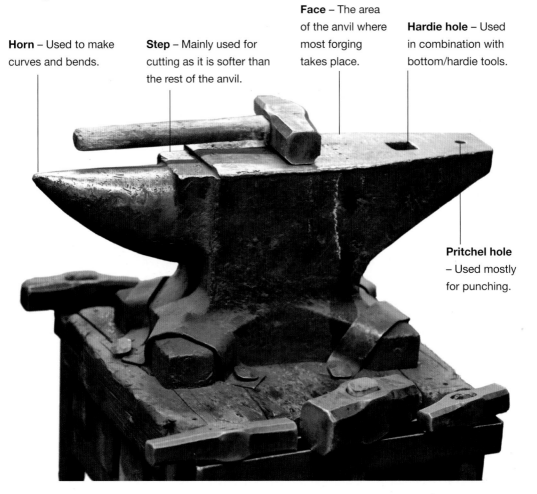

Horn – Used to make curves and bends.

Step – Mainly used for cutting as it is softer than the rest of the anvil.

Face – The area of the anvil where most forging takes place.

Hardie hole – Used in combination with bottom/hardie tools.

Pritchel hole – Used mostly for punching.

USES OF AN ANVIL

The flat surface of an anvil can serve as a convenient workspace for sketching out temporary designs or marking precise measurements to guide the forging process.

ANVIL, HAMMER & TONGS

When setting up an anvil, a wooden block can be placed underneath to provide a stable base. This also allows for the attachment of straps or loops to hold various tools so they are within easy reach during forging.

ANVILS COME IN DIFFERENT STYLES
Anvils come in many styles, from the London pattern to the Swedish or Sawyer anvil with no horn or heel. Each is adapted for its area of production or task, such as a chain makers' anvil or a small jeweller's anvil.

USING THE HORN
The horn can be used to bend
or scroll a bar. It can also be
used for heavy forging.

Above:
BLACKSMITH'S HELPER
The blacksmith's helper
is a tool that enables the
user to hold both a top and
bottom insert as if using a
top and bottom tool, while
also having a free hand to
hammer on the workpiece.

Right: BENDING DOG
This tool sits in the hardie
hole and is held in place by
the anvil, allowing you to
apply force to the bar and
create an accurate bend.

ANVIL TOOLS

All listed tools are made from high-carbon steel (tool steel) and are heat-treated.

Hardie Tool

Hardie tools, otherwise known as bottom tools, consist of a square shank that fits into the hardie hole on the anvil. The term 'hardie' tool refers to a hot cut bottom tool. Other bottom tools are referred to by their function. For example, a common tool is a fuller that is normally matched with the same-radius top tool fuller. Used in combination, you can pinch and isolate material, allowing for a faster rate of material movement. The swage is the inverse of the fuller tool. When both top and bottom tools are used in unison they can shape a bar to a desired size or be used as a die to make finials, along with other uses.

An additional use of the hardie hole is to securely hold a custom-made jig for a forging process, as it allows you to keep your hands free, and removes the need to hold the jig or have it in a vice farther away from the forge.

Another useful bottom tool is a bending tool. The hardie hole's square shape stops the tool from twisting, while the weight of the anvil acts as an anchor, allowing you to apply a high amount of force to bend the hot steel.

Fuller

A fuller is a tool used by a blacksmith to create a groove or channel into a bar that is being worked on. The groove can be used for a variety of purposes, such as reducing weight or adding decorative elements.

Swage

A swage is a tool used to shape or form metal into a particular shape or size. Swages are commonly used in combination with a fuller to produce specific shapes or designs in the metal being worked.

AXE DRIFT
This tool is used to hold an axe during the forging process to avoid collapsing the sides of the axe and to help forge the end shape of the eye.

FULLER

Fullers can come in various shapes and sizes, but they generally have a rounded or square profile and are used to create specific shapes or designs in metalwork.

BLOCK BRUSH

A butcher's block brush can be used between forging steps to clean scale and burnish the surface of the metal.

SCROLLING PREFORM
Scrolling preforms are used
to help create a consistent,
repeatable scroll.

FULLER
A bottom fuller can be used
in tandem with a top tool to
pinch or draw out material.

Far left:
RECTANGLE PUNCH
A rectangle punch is used
to create elongated square-
cornered holes in metal.
These are often created to fit
tenons or other components
that require a precise fit

Left: SQUARE PUNCH
A square punch is used to
punch square-shaped holes
into a piece of metal. The
size of the hole is determined
by how deep the material is
punched through.

Right: SLITTER
A slitter is used in instances
when removing large
amounts of material would
be detrimental to the
structural integrity of the
object. It punches out a small
amount of material, allowing
it to be hot drifted to size,
thereby preserving the
thickness of material.

PRITCHEL HOLE & HARDIE HOLE

A pritchel hole is a round hole in an anvil. The square hole is the hardie hole. Both are designed to accommodate other tools in the blacksmithing process.

Hot Cut

A hot cut is a bottom tool used by blacksmiths to cut hot metal. It consists of a chisel-like blade that is struck with a hammer to cut the metal.

Bending Tool

This square-shanked tool often has a heavy round bar bent into a U shape to allow for consistent bends when making items such as S hooks or any object with a bend.

Jig

A jig is a tool that holds the workpiece in a specific position to allow for consistent and repeatable results, such as a scrolling jig for creating consistent scrolls.

Pritchel Hole

The pritchel hole is located near the heel of the anvil and is multipurpose. It can be used with a holdfast to secure a workpiece or for punching holes, allowing for the slug of material to be removed, before the hole is drifted to size. Note that a punch larger than the pritchel hole may get stuck.

This is where drifts come into play as they are a set size and can be made smaller than the pritchel hole. For operations requiring a larger hole to be punched, once a hole has been punched or drifted to the largest that the pritchel can allow for, you can move to the hardie hole to finish the job. Alternatively, a bottom tool can be made to help achieve the desired size.

Punch

A punch is a tool used to remove a section of steel from a bar to create a hole of the desired shape and size. These tools are tapered and shaped for the job.

The basic punches are: round punch, square punch and slitter punch. The first two are just different shapes, but the function of the slitter is slightly different, as it does not remove steel; instead, it cuts it, allowing for less steel to be removed. The effect of this is normally a swell around the hole. Often, this is a desired forging aesthetic and it also serves a function: in removing less material, the steel is left stronger as there is more material around the hole.

Above & right:
FLATTER
A twisted forged-handle flatter (above). The metal handle allows for the vibration of hitting the tool to be reduced while also offering a longer working life than that of a wooden handle. Here (right) you can see the smith holding the flatter in place while the sticker hits the tool in a rhythmic manner.

Drift

Drifts are used to achieve a consistent size after punching a hole. They are typically made from mild steel with a forged or ground taper that matches the desired finished dimensions of the hole. Drifts are considered a consumable tool, designed for a single job, but they can also be made from high-carbon steel for increased durability at the cost of longer production time.

Flatter

This is a handled tool similar to a hammer but with a large, flat side with radiused edges. The reverse side is square and is struck by a hammer to smooth and flatten steel, normally at the end of the forging stage, to create a smooth, consistent surface.

Holdfast

A holdfast is a clamping tool made from a round bar that fits into the pritchel hole of your anvil. Once hammered down, it creates a snug fit that allows you to securely pinch down on a workpiece, freeing up your hands for forging without having to hold the piece.

Right:
TOOLS OF THE TRADE
This picture shows a selection
of commonly used tools
within blacksmithing laid
out on a metal workbench.
The hide mallet in the centre
is used for hammer blows
that don't mark the steel.
There is also a range of other
hammers, such as cross peens
and a ball peen hammer.
There are various tongs on
display: square bolt tongs,
round hollow bit tongs, rivet
tongs, flat bit bolt tongs and
scrolling tongs, as well as jigs,
bending tools and top tools,
such as a flatter and a fuller.

Overleaf:
FILES & RASPS
A selection of wood and
metal working files and rasps
is needed in a workshop to
refine shapes in both wood
and metal for the making or
repairing of tools, and for
commission work.

THE FORGE

There are many options to consider when choosing your forge. When starting out, the most versatile type would be either a bottom blast or a side blast forge, as the area of heat can be controlled precisely. The same cannot be said for gas forges, which will heat anything placed inside the whole length of the chamber and cannot easily be shortened or lengthened.

I N THIS CHAPTER, both traditional and modern gas forges and their potential fuels will be discussed. For gas forges, the fuel used is propane, as it can reach the temperature needed for fire welding. Traditional-style forges have multiple options for fuel: coal and a refined version of coal called coke. Another, lesser used, fuel is charcoal.

TYPES OF FORGE
The benefits of the forges and fuels are listed below, along with their drawbacks.

Traditional Forge
Traditional forges are made from cast iron or fabricated from sheet and plate steel. They have a metal hood to extract the smoke and fumes from the fire. This must be connected up to a flue system to extract the smoke and fumes from the workplace. Both styles of traditional forges use a fan system that blows air into the centre of the fire. This air stokes and increases the temperature of the fire.

It is important to note that while burning, the impurities in both coal and coke will melt down into klinker. This has to be cleared out of the forge throughout the day to ensure that there is an unimpeded pathway to the centre of the fire and the air outlet is not blocked.

To set up either of these forges, sand can be used to give a base to the fire and protect the bottom of the forge from the extreme heat. When filling the bed of the forge with this sand, care should be taken to avoid covering any air holes.

Side Blast Forge
This style of forge uses a tuyere iron – a water-cooled pipe connected to a water reserve behind the forge that allows air to pass through to the heart of the fire. The size of the workable area within the forge can be controlled by adding or removing sand to increase the size of the fire. The klinker that is formed tends to sit below the air intake as it melts, and flows down to the cooler part of the fire.

TRADITIONAL FORGE
A traditional brick forge powered by a large set of bellows positioned behind.
These feed air to the fire through a tuyere iron or clay pipe.

Fuel Types

The choice of fuel used controls the cleanliness of the fire and its potential to build up slag. Below are listed the various perks of using each type of fuel. All are lit using paper to light some kindling. The chosen fuel is then raked over the kindling to be ignited.

COAL

Coal is the dirtiest forging fuel of the three types. If using it, you will first need to build a small mound before igniting it. Let the fire heat up to a forging temperature and then poke your workpiece into it, creating a tunnel for your material. Coal has a tendency to stick together due to the build-up of slag from the unrefined coal. Thanks to the high amount of impurities it contains, it will also cause a faster build-up of klinker than any other forging fuel.

COKE

Coke is a refined version of coal. When using it, the forge is set up in a similar way to that of the coal forge. While forging, it is important to keep the coke built up in a small mound; in so doing, you provide enough fuel to keep the fire at forging temperature. While this is a refined version of coal, some klinker will still be produced in the forge, though the amount will be less than that produced by coal.

CHARCOAL

A charcoal forge is set up and maintained in the same way as ones that use the above fuels. Compared to coal and coke, charcoal is very pure, which means that there is very low production of klinker. The major downside of using this fuel is that you will get through it very quickly, since it burns faster than both coal and coke.

Above & left:
ADDING FUEL
Fuel should be added behind the fire rather than directly on top as this would reduce the heat of the fire. Placing it behind allows it to dry out and preheat before it is added to the fire. This method also reduces the risk of popping coals. A fire rake can be used to keep the fire built up and the hot coals where you want them.

Left: COAL STORE
The coal or coke shown here is in a mass coal store. A coal scuttle or short-handled shovel can be used to transfer the fuel to the forge.

Below left: KLINKER
Klinker is the fused impurities and sand produced by burning coal or coke. This has to be removed from the fire to keep the fire and metal clean.

Below right: BURNT COKE
Burnt coke will often be lighter in weight and ashy white in colour. It can be used to help start a fire as it has been completely dried.

Above:
JAPANESE SWORDSMITH
A modern-day Japanese swordsmith in the process of fire welding a billet of steel together under a powerhammer. In the background is a traditional Fuigo box bellows, which is pumped back and forth to push air into the forge.

Left:
BOTTOM BLAST FORGE
A bottom blast forge powered by a hand-cranked blower. These types of fan are great for portable forges and unpowered workshops.

This can build up to the point where it covers the air outlet, which will dramatically affect the airflow. This will be indicated by the fire cooling regardless of airflow. The issue can be fixed by letting the fire cool and then using a fire poker to lift the klinker out of the fire, which can then be relit and the work can continue.

This type of forge offers excellent control over the fire through its adjustable airflow and fire size. However, one downside is its weight. These forges are typically made of heavy cast or fabricated materials, which makes them immobile and requires them to be connected to a flue system.

Bottom Blast Forge
This forge type is characterized by the airflow entering the fire from below the forge. These forges come in a variety of constructions, from heavy cast components to smaller, more portable designs. This portability is where the bottom blast forge excels over the side blast forge. Additionally, it has the ability to provide very precise and small heating, using the same

method as the side blast forge. However, one drawback to this forge is that the air holes at the base can become blocked faster than the air outlet of the side blast forge. To remove the blockages, a fire poker can be used to lift and remove the klinker once the fire has cooled.

Gas Forge
The use of a gas forge in blacksmithing offers the greatest mobility compared to traditional forges due to its smaller size. Moreover, propane fuel provides extended forging time and is lighter in weight than coal or coke. However, it is important to note that gas forges tend to produce more scale than traditional forges, and there is an added risk when using a compressed gas bottle.

Below & overleaf:
GAS FORGE
This gas forge is being used for the batch production of an item by utilizing the forge's ability to hold an accurate set heat, allowing for the smith to work without worry of burning the stock in the fire.

Opposite:
HAND-CRANKED FORGE
Puyallup, Washington, USA. A young woman blacksmith hand-cranks a blower on a portable forge.

It is crucial to maintain a safe distance between the forge and fuel sources. A flash back arrestor should also be installed on the fuel line to act as a failsafe in case of any accidents. Additionally, the potential dangers associated with working with a gas forge should be researched before purchasing one. All gas forges should be used in places with adequate ventilation.

Venturi Forge

A gas forge that uses a Venturi air system doesn't rely on electricity, which means it is more versatile than the forced air system. Another benefit is that in the event of a power outage, airflow to the gas forge will be maintained and it will still run.

The Venturi effect is a phenomenon in which the velocity of a fluid increases as it flows through a constricted section of a pipe, resulting in a decrease in pressure. By constricting the airflow through a small nozzle, the air velocity is increased, allowing for more efficient combustion of the fuel gas and resulting in a hotter flame. The temperature in the forge can be

Above:
FIRE WELDING TEMPERATURE
A billet of steel composed of layers of differing carbon content being brought up to fire welding temperature in a gas forge. The surface of the steel is coated in molten borax flux, which helps to reduce the build-up of scale and improves the chance of fusing the layers.

adjusted by controlling the amount of air that enters the burner. A downside to this style of forge is that it tends to have lower fuel efficiency, which can result in higher fuel consumption. However, this forge is extremely versatile, and can be used for a variety of forging processes.

Forced Air Forge

The use of a forced air gas forge allows for more precise temperature control as air is forced into the burner by means of a fan. This method also allows for higher temperatures to be achieved compared to the Venturi effect.

The risk of this type of forge is that the fan may fail, leading to potential safety hazards. Thus, proper safety measures should be taken when setting up and using this type of forge. Indeed, this advice holds true for all types of forges and tools in the workshop.

FIRING UP A FORGE

Opposite left & below: The first step of setting up the forge fire is to prepare some scrunched-up paper and kindling. Next, clear the air vent of sand and coals.

Opposite right: Arrange the kindling and paper in the forge, then light it.

Right: Once the fire is established, turn on the fan.

Below: As the fan gets going, add dry coke or coal around the edges of the fire, allowing an exit for the smoke. Keep adding fuel until the fire is fully lit.

Overleaf: Once the fire is fully lit, keep the fan set to low to allow the fire to slowly come up to heat, to avoid hot spots. This can take 10–15 minutes.

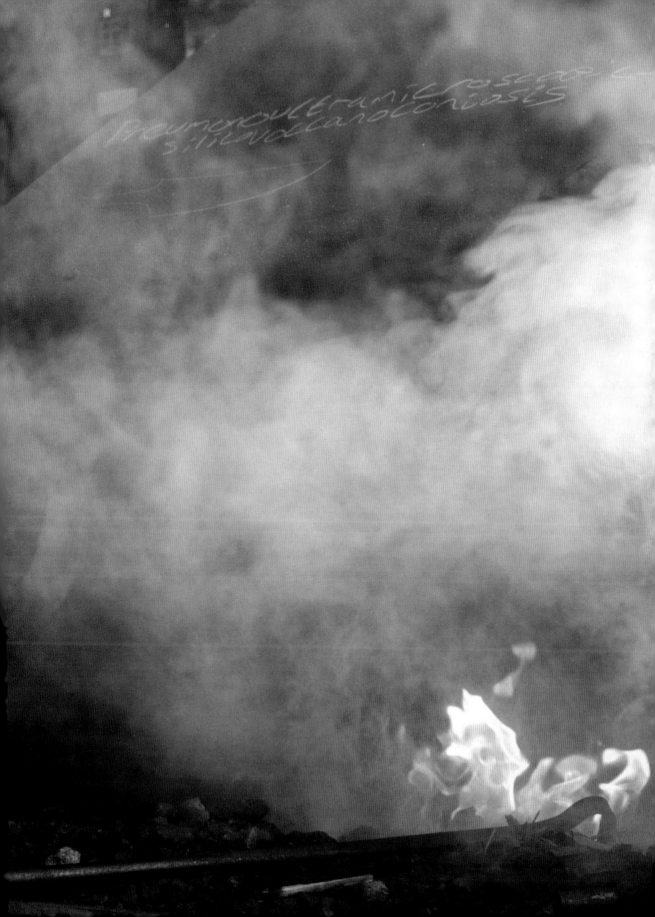

Maintenance

Here are some basic maintenance techniques for different types of forges:

Side blast forge: The back bosh should be kept filled at all times to prevent the tuyere iron from melting. The forge will need to be rebedded occasionally. When you do this, reshape the divot around the air outlet according to the desired fire size, leaving enough room for klinker to settle and form under the tuyere iron.

Bottom blast forge: Over time, the heat generated by the forge will cause oxidation of the air outlet, resulting in the need for periodic replacement. Additionally, sand and debris from the fire will accumulate within the outlet, potentially impeding airflow to the fire. It is important to regularly remove this debris to ensure adequate airflow. The bed of the forge will also require adjustment during use to maintain the desired size and shape of the fire.

Gas forge: Over time, the refractory lining of the forge will deteriorate and need to be replaced. It's important to use the same materials as the original lining or else an alternative recommended by the manufacturer. When working with refractory materials, it's essential to wear a respirator and gloves to protect against fine particulate. All gas connections should be inspected according to the safety regulations in your country. If you're using a forced air forge, check the fan to ensure it's functioning properly.

BELLOWS
A large set of bellows is being used with a portable forge to provide ample airflow to the fire. Wet rags have been placed across the metal air outlet of the bellows to protect it and the wooden bellows from overheating and burning.

FORGEABLE METALS

The most commonly used metals for forging are iron and its alloys, copper and its alloys, and types of steel. It is crucial to check the specifications of your chosen metal. For example, steel alloys with more than 1 per cent carbon content can be difficult to forge, and those with a carbon content of 1.7-3 per cent become cast iron, which cannot be forged.

DIFFERENT METALS

Here is a basic list of metals for forging and their various properties.

Mild Steel

Mild steel (carbon content of 0.05–0.25 per cent) is the most commonly used steel in blacksmithing today as it is stronger than iron and softer than higher-carbon steels. It is used for general forging and in projects that do not require the strength or the resilience of a higher-carbon steel. It also is lower in cost than both high-carbon steel and iron.

High-carbon Steel

The higher carbon content (0.6–1 per cent) of high-carbon steel makes it useful for creating impact tools, knives and springs, among other uses. Each alloy has different properties and excels in different areas. For example, 15N20 contains 0.75 per cent carbon and 2 per cent nickel, this latter giving it great corrosive resistance. Compared to O1 tool steel, which has a carbon content of 0.855–1 per cent, it also contains 0.4–0.6 per cent tungsten, resulting in higher hardness but lower corrosion resistance than 15N20 steel. Therefore, choose the appropriate steel for the job based on its properties. A few high-carbon steel types and their uses are listed below:

• 1095 (0.95 per cent carbon): Knife steel
• 01 tool steel (0.85–1 per cent carbon): Tool steel (punches/hot cut)

Above: WROUGHT IRON
Wrought iron can be identified by cutting halfway into a bar and bending it until it fails. As the metal fails, the grain structure of the wrought iron will be visible through the tear, as shown as above.

• 15N20 (0.75 per cent carbon): Knife steel can be used with 15N20 to make pattern-welded steel.

Wrought Iron

Wrought iron differs from steel in that its carbon content is often very low, at around 0.1 per cent. In addition, it contains around 2 per cent slag. While the slag can cause the metal to split apart when worked at low temperatures, it acts as a flux and helps fuse the iron back together. The more it is worked, the more consolidated the iron becomes, and the more slag is worked out, resulting in a slightly harder metal.

Overheating the wrought iron during forging can cause massive grain growth and lead to cracks. Steps can be taken to reduce the grain growth formation and are described in the heat treatment chapter.

Above: MILD STEEL
Mild steel is the most general-purpose iron alloy used by blacksmiths, being easy to forge and readily available.

Opposite: HIGH-CARBON STEEL
The high hardness achieved through quenching makes this steel suitable for a variety of applications, such as hammers, knives and anvils.

Opposite: COPPER
Copper has been used throughout history for making cooking pots, since copper transfers heat very well. To be food-safe, a tin coating is applied to the inside to stop acid from reacting with the coppper.

Wrought iron is often used in heritage work to replace like for like in a repair.

Cast Iron

Cast iron is any iron-carbon alloy that contains over 2 per cent of carbon. This high carbon content makes it brittle and unsuitable for forging.

Copper

Copper is a relatively soft metal that can be forged very easily. When handling heated copper you must use tongs as the heat conductivity of the metal is much higher than that of steel or iron. It can be forged once it is glowing bright red as it is extremely soft compared to steel. Avoid overheating it; if you heat it to a bright yellow then you run the risk of either moving too much material or melting the copper.

CAST IRON KEYS
Cast iron is popular for the mass production of objects such as keys as the casting method allows for easy replication.

BRASS DOOR KNOCKER
Brass is a popular metal for ornamental purposes due to its ease of casting, which is facilitated by its lower melting point compared to that of steel or copper. While brass cannot be easily formed through forging, casting allows for intricate and beautiful designs to be created.

Brass

Brass is an alloy made of copper and zinc. Heating brass releases dangerous zinc oxide fumes, which makes it important to work in a well-ventilated area. Overheating brass can also cause the zinc to vaporize out, resulting in weakened brass that easily crumbles.

WARNING:
If using scrap steel such as car springs, be aware that they may have undetectable flaws that may lead to failure of the end product, which could in turn result in injury.

HEAT TREATMENT

Heat treatment is an essential process in the making of hardened steel tools such as knives, hot cuts, punches and hammers, to name but a few. The process involves many steps to reach a successful result, each of which must be followed precisely. This chapter outlines a relatively simple method suitable for a basic set-up.

WHILE HEAT TREATMENT is a very involved process that can require specialized machinery, a rougher method can be used with a basic forge set-up. The end result can greatly differ in usefulness, but while learning the basics of blacksmithing, the rough-and-ready heat treatment process will be adequate.

WHAT IS HEAT TREATMENT?

Heat treatment of steel or other metals and materials such as aluminium and glass is a process that involves heating and then cooling a chosen material to precise temperatures for a set amount of time for each stage. This serves to change the microstructure of the material and produce an end result with the desired properties. This will be explained in depth below.

The desired end result of heat treatment of a knife blade, for example, is for it to hold a sharp edge and not bend. The downside is that hardening will cause the blade to become brittle. The hardening is created by quenching the blade. This having been done, some of the hardness must now be removed to bring it back to a usable blade, using a process called tempering.

THE SCIENCE

During the heat treatment process, one important step is heating the steel to a temperature above 725°C (1,337°F). At this temperature, the steel loses its magnetic properties and will not regain them until it cools back down below this point. This is due to the crystal structure of iron changing from body-centered cubic (BCC) to face-centered cubic (FCC) as a result of the heat. This change in structure creates a denser-packed crystal structure (FCC), allowing carbon atoms to move more freely than at lower temperatures. When quenching the steel, the carbon atoms effectively become frozen in place throughout the material, resulting in a hard but brittle microstructure known as martensite.

This process gives rise to the three major phases of iron: austenite, cementite and martensite.

- **Austenite**: This is normally formed above 725°C (1,337°F), when the structure becomes FFC and non-magnetic. It can also be achieved through alloying with nickel and other elements, leading to austenitic stainless steel.
- **Cementite** (iron carbide): This is normally classed as a ceramic in its pure form.
- **Martensite**: The carbon has been evenly distributed throughout the steel, creating a fibrous structure.

The major influence on the end result is the carbon content of the steel, and whether or not it is allowed to reach each stage fully. This being said, the soak time during heating and the speed of the quench through the correct medium both play pivotal roles.

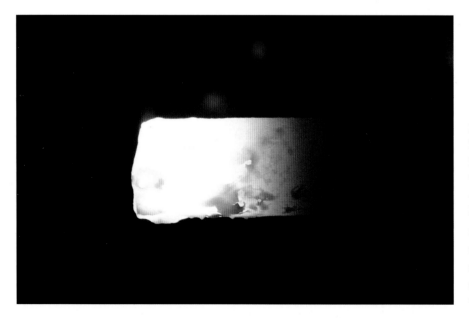

Left and opposite:
HEATING METAL FOR FORGING
When heating steel and various other metals, they will glow to indicate how hot the metal has become during the process. The glow comes from the heat exciting the metal's electrons, giving off visible light.

Bright yellow indicates a temperature of around 1,038–1,093°C (1,900–2,000°F).

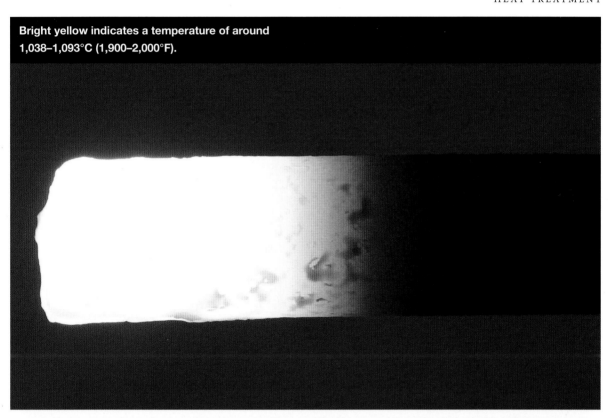

Bright orange-yellow indicates a temperature of 982°C (1,800°F).

Dull orange indicates a temperature of 760°C (1,400°F).

Cherry red indicates a temperature of 704°C (1,300°F).

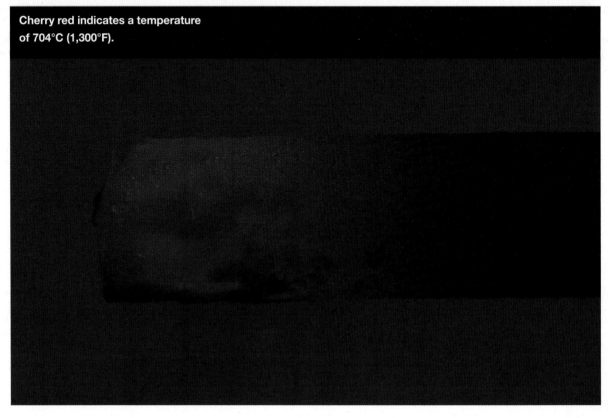

Dull red indicates a temperature of 649°C (1,200°F).

A slight red glow indicates a temperature of 593°C (1,100°F).

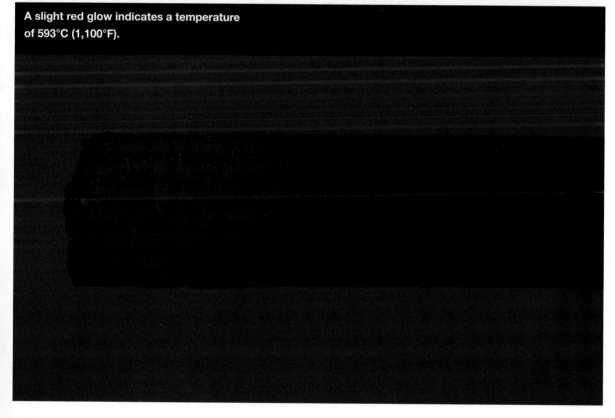

Annealing

The purpose of annealing is to improve the grain structure of the metal. This is done through slowly heating the material to the required temperature and allowing it to soak, then finishing with a slow cool-down. Often, this can be done by bringing it to its critical temperature around 725°C (1,337°F) in the forge, holding it at that temperature for a set amount of time, then turning off the forge with the metal still in it, allowing both to cool down slowly. If done correctly, the result is that the internal stresses of the metal have been relieved and the metal is more ductile.

Normalizing

Normalizing is similar to annealing. Not all metals can be normalized, but the main ones used by blacksmiths can: steels, iron, cast iron, brass, aluminium and copper. In essence, you are normalizing the grain structure of the metal, which relieves the internal stresses. In contrast to annealing, normalized metal retains more toughness, meaning that the heat-treated part can withstand impacts better. For example, a mild steel striking hammer or tool hammer could be made with a normalized head to reduce damage to top tools. The normalized head will also wear evenly and last longer than an annealed or non-normalized version.

Tempering

Tempering the steel is the final step in the heat treatment process. It reduces that brittleness and the internal stresses in the metal caused by quenching. This step again involves heating and quenching, however the temperature range is much lower – from 176°C to 388°C (349–730°F). For this step to have a strong effect on the metal it must be heated to the chosen temperature, held there for about an hour (this time may vary for different metals) and then quenched. The lower the chosen temperature, the more brittle and hard the end result will be. A knife, for instance, would be tempered at around 200–220°C (392–428°F).

Flame Hardening

This is an example of a localized heat treatment, where only a specific part of the metal is heated and treated. For instance, the blade edge of a knife could be heated above its critical temperature using a gas torch and then

HARDENED STEEL
This photograph shows the scale formation of hardened steel.

quenched, resulting in only the edge being hardened. The torch can then be used again to temper the blade by setting the flame low so as not to overheat the steel.

Decarburization

Decarburization happens when the steel is heated to above critical temperature while in the presence of an oxidizing atmosphere. As the carbon comes into solution with the iron, the carbon will react with the oxidizing atmosphere and leach out, reducing the percentage of the carbon in the steel. This is usually an undesired end result, though the method can be used to remove carbon from steel if needed.

EVERY METAL IS DIFFERENT

Make sure you check the specifications of the metal being used so you know the correct way to heat treat it. It is also important to wear appropriate PPE during the quenching stage to avoid burns and other injuries. Use extra caution with air hardening steels because if you accidentally quench them, there is a chance that the internal stresses may cause them to crack apart or explode under the stress. Stay safe.

Quenching

Quenching is the process of rapidly cooling metal after it has been heated above the critical temperature. This freezes the grain structure of the material and changes its mechanical properties.

There are many ways to quench metals and each has their benefits and downsides. The basic ones are water, oil and air quenches. The water quench runs the risk of creating a steam jacket around the metal and causing uneven quenching. This could potentially lead to a crack forming due to the stresses involved. Oil is slower than water, meaning it is less likely to over-stress the material and cause a crack, but it is to be noted that it is flammable so leave the metal submerged until it has fully cooled. Some steels are air hardening and so can be heated to a critical temperature and left to cool in the air. These require a different method of annealing and normalizing. This will be touched upon later.

Below is a list of quenching media that can be used. For best results, follow the heat treatment guide for the steel that you are using, which can often be found online or via your steel merchant. If the metal has not been annealed prior to this step then the metal may warp from the internal stress.

• **Water:** A very fast quench that may over-stress some steels. It is non-flammable so there's no fire risk when quenching steel.

• **Oil:** A medium-speed quench offering reliable results. Different types of oil can be used to speed or slow the cooling rates. Common ones are vegetable or canola oil. Professional oils can also be bought. Care is needed when quenching in oil as it is flammable.

• **Air:** This quenching method may involve leaving an air-hardenable steel in room temperature air to harden or using compressed air to rapidly cool the metal. It is often a slow quench and is likely to affect the mechanical properties. However, if the metal is placed between two thick plates of aluminium, and compressed air is forced through the gap, rapid cooling may be achieved. This method has the additional benefit of the metal being held straight while cooling.

• **Brine:** Comprising a mixture of water and salt, brine is the fastest quench media. Due to the presence of the salt, it inhibits the formation of excess air bubbles when it comes in contact with the quenched steel. The percentage of salt for quenching in brine is between 5 and 7 per cent.

Water is the fastest method for quenching.

PROJECTS

The projects within this section make use of multiple techniques. These can be practised separately or as part of the projects. All of them require the use of a forge and anvil, and some additional tools, which are listed for each project.

MAKING A LEAF PENDANT

The forged leaf is a small, decorative item that can be made in a short amount of time, while also displaying a broad range of different skills.

This project will cover basic techniques such as forward and reverse tapering and learning how to accurately isolate material using the anvil to forge set downs, finishing with forging the tapered stem of the leaf into a scrolled end. Once completed, the decorative leaf can be attached to a pendant, light pull or keyring.

Materials:
- 12mm (0.5in) round bar, 36cm (14in) in length
- Beeswax, cloth rag or a scrap piece of newspaper

Tools:
- Ball peen hammer
- Wire brush
- Pliers or tongs

Skills and techniques used:
- Tapering (forward and reverse)
- Setting down
- Scrolling

Key notes:
- As the project progresses, potential problems can present themselves due to varying thicknesses of materials used.

- Watch your heat, or you could burn your project.

- As you're forging your leaf, try to keep it attached to the bar stock if possible. This will mean you don't require any tongs in order to hold the project while you're working on it.

The completed leaf pendant.

The material: 10mm (0.4in) round bar.

1. Forging the tip

Heat the round bar to a bright orange to yellow heat so that you can efficiently move material (A). Place the glowing tip at the far edge of the anvil and strike it at a 45-degree angle with a ball peen hammer, rotating the rod as you do so. By retaining the angle during hammering and rotating the rod, a short taper will begin to form, eventually creating a steep point at the end of the bar (B).

Key tools

Some of the key tools
needs for this project:

   Ball peen hammer

   Leather gloves

   Pliers and tongs

   Apron

2. Set down, before and after

Place the newly formed taper point over the edge of the anvil, bringing the angle of the bar up so that its edge can bite into the bar stock (A). Hammer half-on, half-off the anvil to force the edge into the bar, creating a set down (B).

A

B

3. Working the sides

Rotate the bar through 90 degrees and repeat. Keep working the two sides until the stem is fairly thin (5–6mm/0.2–0.24in). When finished, there should be a square section with a gradual taper that is pointing towards the hand that is holding the bar.

4. Forging a set down to finish

Working the same two sides and keeping the tip of the bar over the edge of the anvil, draw down the bar into a smooth, gradual taper, creating the full length of the leaf's stem (A). By moving the bar to the near edge of the anvil, you can create a set down at the point where you wish to terminate the stem. Continue forging, creating a reverse taper up to what will become the main leaf, leaving the thickness around 3mm (0.12in) (B & C).

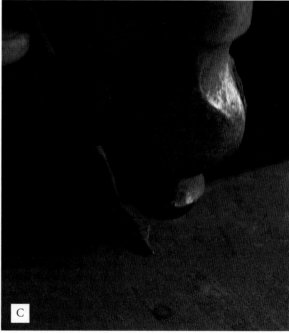

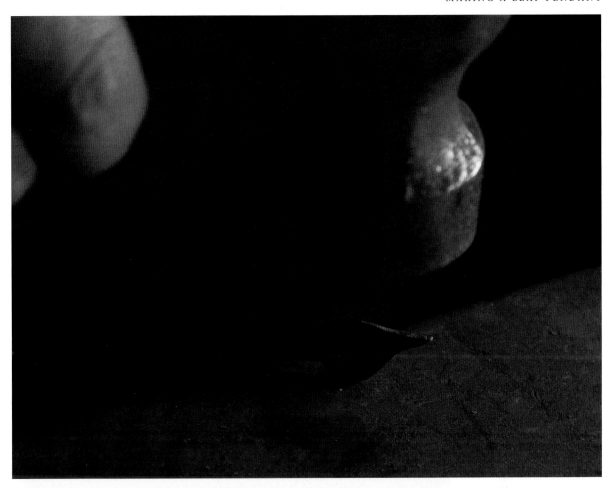

5. Flattening the leaf

Forge down with angled hammer blows on one side only of the raised edge of the isolated material from step 2. Next, forge straight down, spreading the leaf material until it is around 4mm (0.15in) in thickness. Now use the ball peen side of a hammer to carefully hit either side of the flattened material, creating a central ridge for your leaf.

6. Light hammer blows

Temperature control is key here – the material for the stem may be overworked if the forging process is done when the bar is below a bright orange heat, putting it at risk of breakage. However, light finishing hammer blows can be made in order to texture the leaf when the material is a cherry or dull red.

7. Side forging

At this point, take a moment to address any rough edges to your leaf. These can be forged back into the main body of material at a dull orange, using light blows. Then you can place the leaf face-up and use a ball peen hammer to make any necessary adjustments.

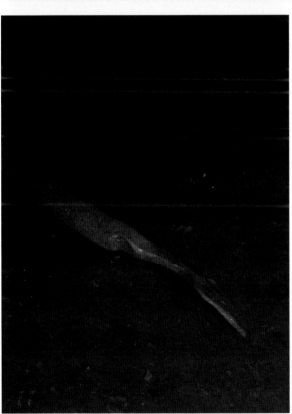

8. Angled forging of stem

Taking care not to bend or hammer the main leaf, forge each corner of the stem down to change the bar from a square to an octagonal shape (A). Keep forging down the raised edges until the bar becomes round and textured (B). Brushing with a wire brush when the material is at a cherry red stage (C) will smooth the surface further.

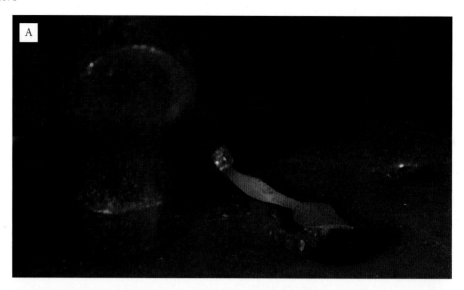

9. Scrolling and separating

Using a pair of pliers or scrolling tongs, bend the stem of the leaf once the material is a bright orange. The end should touch the underside of the leaf, and for the best effect, the curve should mimic that of the Golden Ratio found in the natural world (A).

Heat the leaf to a bright orange then, while holding the leaf in a pair of pliers or tongs (B), twist the bar until it breaks off in a safe termination (C).

10. Brushing
The leaf can now be held and brushed with a wire brush, burnishing the surface ready for wax.

10. Finishing stages
Let the leaf warm up by holding it in tongs either in the flames or on the coals (A), but do not let it reach a glowing red stage. Test the temperature by touching some beeswax to the metal – the temperature is correct if the wax does not smoke excessively (B).

11. Polishing

You are looking for the wax to coat the material in a thin layer – otherwise, the wax is at risk of igniting and creating a fireball. Once you've applied a thin layer of wax to your leaf, wait for it to cool down before polishing it with a cloth rag or a scrap piece of newspaper.

MAKING A PUNCH

This project will focus on material control, smoothly forging each stage to completion and leaving you with a quality tool. It will also be the first in which heat treatment techniques are used, including hardening by oil quench, annealing and tempering.

Materials:
- 20mm (0.75in) round high carbon (spring or tool steel) bar, 18cm (7in) in length
- Quenching oil

Tools:
- Hollow bit tongs
- Ball peen hammer
- Rasp (or belt/angle grinder)
- Wire brush

Skills and techniques used:
- Tapering
- Material control and refinement
- Heat treatment
- Surface finishing

Key notes:
- Avoid bringing the steel to a bright yellow temperature. This can cause carbon to leach out and potentially burn the steel, which would require you to start again with new material.

- A belt or angle grinder can be used to smooth and round the punch instead of rasping it to shape.

- A bad temper can be very dangerous, so make sure to check for cracks.

- Finished size: 19cm/7.5in, taper from 20mm to 5mm (0.75 to 0.2in).

The completed punch.

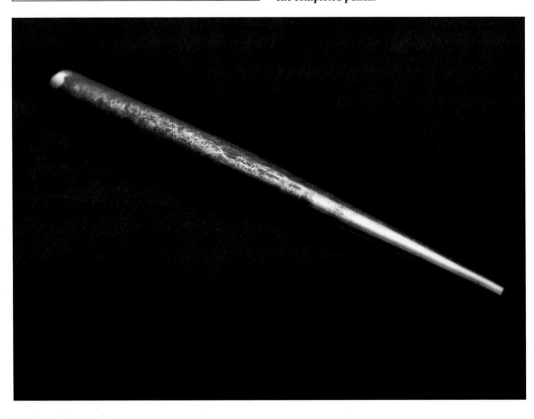

The material: 20mm (0.75in) round high-carbon bar.

1. Forging the bar

Heat the bar to a bright orange, then grasp the bar in the hollow bit tongs. Using a ball peen hammer, start forging two sides into a square bar (A). This will allow you to better keep track of the taper, which will be formed next. Leave 75mm (3in) of the original material at the top of the bar. Once the tip has been shaped into a square, turn it around and forge a sharp taper on the edge (B). By only taking the corners off, you can create a chamfered edge.

2. Forming an octagonal taper

Forge each corner of the square down to form an octagonal shape. Take care to hold the bar straight and keep the forging even, paying special attention to the top part of the heated area where the taper starts, to ensure a higher-quality end result.

3. Finishing the forging

Continue knocking high spots down until the bar looks smooth and round, with an even taper down the length of the punch. Use a wire brush during this process to help to smooth the surface of your punch, especially towards the end of forging.

4. Rasping and wire brushing

Using a rasp and wire brush, file the surface of the punch until smooth. Use the more textured side of the rasp to begin with (A), then use the finer side. Finally, finish with aggressive brushing using the wire brush (B). The metal will oxidize again during the heat treatment, but the smoother it is at this stage, the easier it will be to clean up afterwards. If you have one, a belt grinder or grinder can also be used.

5. Treatment
Heat and cool the punch following the normalizing cycle needed for the steel being used (see the heat treatment chapter).

MAKING A HOT CUT TOOL

A hot cut tool can be used to make a range of tools and artifacts. The difficulty of this project lies more in the heat treatment than the forgework. As with the punch project, controlling the forge temperature is very important – heating too much can remove carbon, while forging at too low a temperature will cause structural flaws in the final product.

Materials:
- 20mm (0.75in) round high carbon (spring or tool steel) bar, 18cm (7in) in length
- Quenching oil

Tools:
- Tongs
- Ball peen hammer
- Rasp (or belt/angle grinder)
- Wire brush

Skills and techniques used:
- Temperature control
- Drawing down material

Key notes:
- As the project progresses, potential problems can present themselves due to the varying thicknesses of the materials used. Watch the amount of heat you use or you could burn your project.

- Once the cutting edge of your hot cut has been heat treated, carefully check to see if any cracks have formed.

- Finished size: cutting edge 35mm/1.4in.

The completed hot cut tool.

The material: 20mm (0.75in) round high carbon bar.

1. Initial heating
Heat the steel bar to a
bright orange, almost
yellow, temperature.

2. Forging techniques

Holding the bar in tongs, use a ball peen hammer to start forging down two sides of the heated area of the bar into an oval/ rectangular cross-section.

3. Creating a taper

Once the thickness is around 3mm, start creating a gradual taper on one end of the bar (A & B). This will become the cutting edge.

A

B

4. Swept edge

Continue forging down two sides of the bar into a gradual taper. As the material is drawn down, it will begin to 'fishtail', or spread out, at the end (A). Forge in one side of the fishtail and tidy up the other side, but don't forge it fully back into itself. Keeping this swept edge allows for a smooth, continuous cut once the completed tool is later used (B).

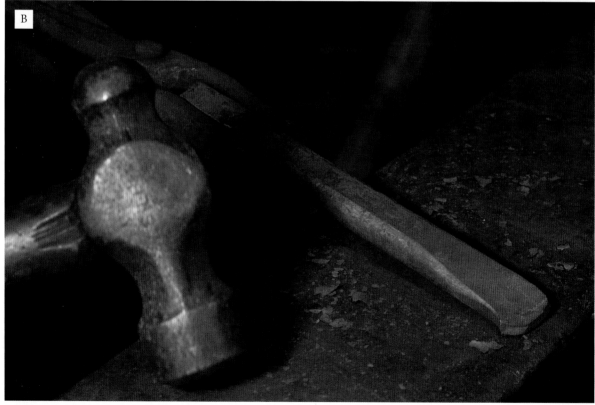

**5. Alternate forging
back and flattening**
Forge the end until it's
around 4mm (0.16in)
thick. While doing this,
the material will start to
bunch together at the
end of the bar. To prevent
cracks from forming,
alternate forging the end
back into the bar and
flattening it.

6. Finishing

While the metal is at a dull orange to cherry red temperature, shape the end of the hot cut tool using a rasp or hammer (A). Further shaping can be carried out with any kind of filing or sanding (B). The finished edge should have an angle of 30 degrees (C).

C

MAKING A BOTTLE OPENER

This project demonstrates the process of accurate punching, followed by drifting and drawing down the punched material using the horn of the anvil. A bottle opener is very simple to forge, but stretching the punched material requires precise forging. You will need to punch a hole accurately from both sides of the material, and ensure you work with the metal at a bright orange temperature to reduce the chance of creating cracks when moving material.

Materials:
- 10mm (0.4in) x 20mm (0.75in) flat bar
- Beeswax, cloth rag or a scrap piece of newspaper

Tools:
- Round faced hammer or ball peen hammer
- Punching tool
- Hollow bit tongs
- Chisel (optional)
- Rawhide or copper mallet
- Wire brush and wax

Skills and techniques used:
- Punching
- Drifting
- Detailing

Key notes:
- The hole that will form your bottle opener does not need to be drifted to increase its size – it can be done using a punch and the anvil horn only, though the result may not be as refined.

- It is important to maintain the thickness of the material around the punched hole – it needs to be sufficiently strong to open a bottle, after all.

- Forge down any sharp edges and thoroughly wire brush the finished piece to ensure a smooth finish that's safe and comfortable to handle.

The completed bottle opener.

1. Making the curves

Heat the bar to a bright orange temperature. Using the horn of the anvil and a round faced hammer or ball peen hammer, forge in a slight fuller on either side of the bar, as shown (A). Regularly flip the bar through 180 degrees to keep the fullers even (B).

2. Punching a hole

Punch a hole in the centre of the bar (A). It is important to quench the punching tool as you work. This will prevent it from overheating and becoming damaged. Do not quench the punching tool if it glows red, though – this can cause it to re-harden and potentially form cracks.

Once the punching tool has hit the bottom of the material and resistance can be felt from the anvil, the bar can be turned over and punched from the other side (B).

3. Expanding the hole

Remove the plug of material using the punching tool (A, B & C). Using your punching tool as a drifting tool and holding the work with tongs, expand the hole you have created using the hardie hole (D & E).

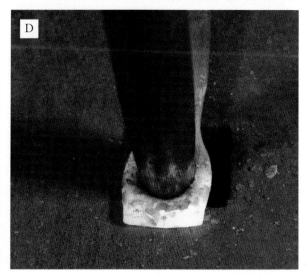

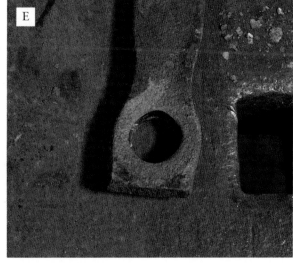

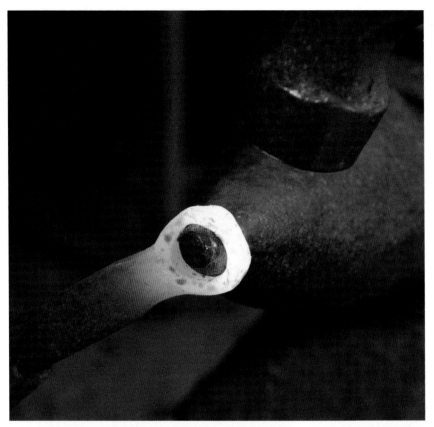

4. Horn work

Fit the hole of the bottle opener over the horn of the anvil. Using the hammer, forge the material thinly on all sides, causing the hole to expand in size. Continue this process until the hole is 25mm (1in) in diameter, allowing it to fit snugly around a bottle cap.

5. Punch a lip

To finish the top of the bottle opener, use a punching tool to punch down a small area of material as shown (A). This will create a lip, which will catch the edge of the bottle cap (B).

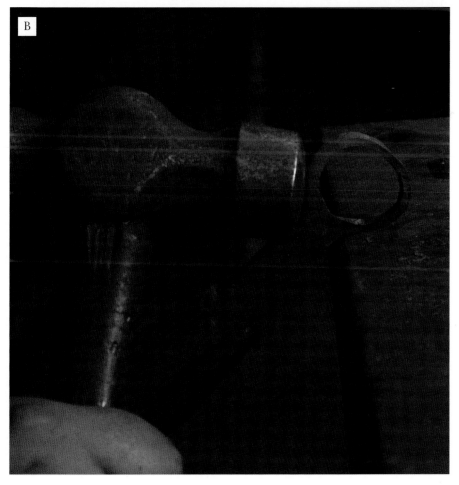

6. Tapered handle

Flip the bottle opener over and heat the handle to red to forge it into shape. It should be forged on two sides only to a gentle taper that expands out towards the bottom of the opener, as shown (A & B).

Before the final shaping of the handle, complete any decorative hammer work or chisel detailing while the material is still flat. The handle can also be left plain if desired.

7. Curving and straightening

Once ready for the final shaping, use a rawhide or copper mallet to create a slight curve in the middle of the handle by hammering over the horn of the anvil (A). To reduce the curvature, lay the handle across the face of the anvil and hit the raised centre in order to lower it (B).

8. Finishing

Use a wire brush while the metal is hot (A) and apply beeswax to finish (B).

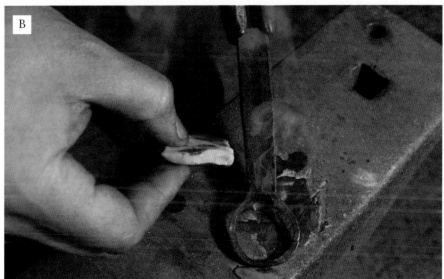

MAKING A FORGED ROSE

Roses are considered a symbol of beauty and love in many cultures, and a beautifully forged one makes a perfect gift. The process of forging such a delicate object will involve both hot and cold work, while also introducing a new material to work with. This project will focus on accuracy and hammer control to end with a natural, organic rose with a smooth hammered or planished surface finish. The forming and texturing of the copper petals will be completed using a few new techniques, such as anticlastic forming, repoussé and chasing.

Materials:
- 2mm/14 gauge copper sheet
- 6mm (¼in) round bar, 30cm (12in) in length
- 10mm (0.4in) round bar

Tools:
- Paper, pen, ruler and scissors
- Scribe
- Hot cut
- Assorted files
- Cross peen hammer and forging hammer
- Rounded chisel tip repoussé punch
- Round punch
- Ball peen hammer
- Vice
- Wire brush and wax
- Hacksaw/angle grinder
- Hot chisel
- Small scrolling pliers/tongs
- Belt grinder
- Drill and drill bit

Additional tools:
- Plasma cutter
- Oxy/acetylene or oxy/propane torch

Skills and techniques used:
- Hammer control
- Anticlastic filming
- Repoussé
- Chasing

Key notes:

Repoussé and chasing

Repoussé means to hammer from the reverse side of the material. Often, this technique makes use of a pitch bowl and pitch to hold the work in place. In this project, however, the forming will happen on a wooden block that will act as a soft surface and allow for relief work. To refine the work done through repoussé, chasing work is then done. Chasing is used to define the form and surface of the front side of the metal sheet. The combination of repoussé and chasing techniques will allow you to create very detailed petals for your rose.

You will need to make some punches (see pages 148–153). You can use water-quenched mild steel to make them since they will only be used on copper – a soft and ductile material. Using mild steel means that they are a quick and affordable alternative to high carbon steel tools. As you use your tools, you will establish your preferred punches and can make these at a later date out of higher-quality, heat-treated steel.

Note on additional tools

These tools have been added to show the other potential ways to tackle this project. The plasma cutter would be used in place of the hot cut to cut the petals out of copper or steel. The pros of doing so are that you can lay out many patterns and cut them out at a much faster rate than by using a hot cut by hand. However, you'll lose time to cleaning dross, the accumulation of waste and foreign matter that is a by-product of the plasma cutting process. The hot cut method, while slower, requires little to no such clean-up – and no expensive plasma cutter.

Access to an oxy/acetylene or oxy/propane gas torch allows for a high level of heat control, which will aid the project but isn't fundamental. If you have a gas torch it can act as a precise and direct heat source, letting you fine-tune the object to your desired specifications.

The completed forged rose with stem.

The materials: copper sheet.

The materials: 6mm (¼in) round bar.

1. Creating a cutting template

Many cutting templates can be found with a simple web search; alternatively, create your own at home. Draw them on paper and cut them out.

2. Tracing the template

Using the chosen cutting templates and a scribe, carefully trace the template for each size of petal on to the copper sheet.

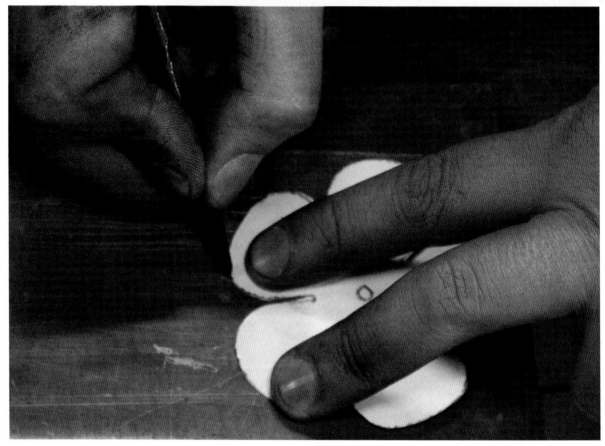

3. Cutting out the petals

Cut out the petals with a hot cut and a sheet of aluminium on top of a steel cutting surface (A). Once cut, use a file to soften the edges and refine the shape of each petal (B).

4. Texturing the petals

Next, texture the petals. Start by using a cross peen hammer to spread and texture the metal evenly across each section, with hammer blows radiating out from the centre (A). A rounded chisel tip repoussé punch can be used to accurately texture or push material in the desired directions (B).

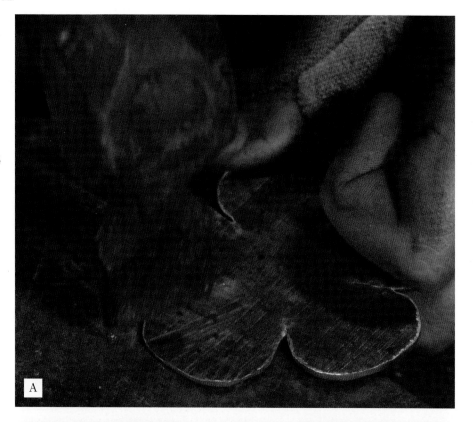

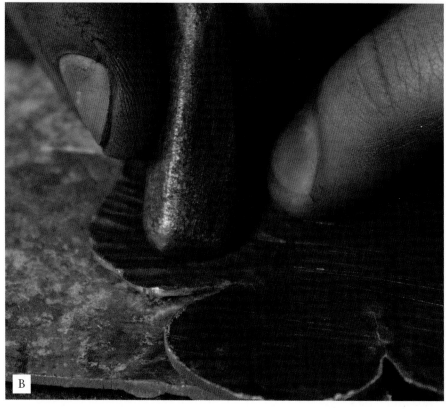

5. Flattening the leaf

Using a ball peen hammer, create a slight hollow in a block of wood. This will be used to shape the petals in combination with a hammer and round punch. Using a wooden block to resist the hammer blows means that it is unlikely to mark the soft copper.

6. Round end punch

A round end punch can be used to further push the copper into the block, thereby tightening up the flower head (A).

Repeat steps 1 to 6 to create the required number of petals. When this has been done, stack the petals to check they fit together neatly (B).

7. Rolling the edges

Using a rounded chisel punch locked in a vice, roll the edges of the petals by hammering down on them over the chisel edge. Aim the hammer blows to land half-on, half-off (A), similar to the setting down process. A mix of hammers can be used to roll the edge: a forging hammer and a cross peen hammer will be useful in thinning out the edge of the material (B).

8. Smoothing the folded edges

Locking the round end punch in a vice, hammer on the folded edges where they have overlapped, in order to smooth them (A) and to allow for a close fit when you place layers of petals together ready for drilling and riveting (B).

9. Forged stem

Next, create a forged stem. Mark 25mm (1in) down on the 6mm (¼in) round bar: this is the area that you'll be heating in order to upset the material (A). Once a swell has been formed, heat the whole end of the bar and fully upset the end to give an even thickness that tapers down to the original stock (B & C). Some time should be taken to forge the end evenly and create an enhanced or sharper taper out of the upset end (D & E).

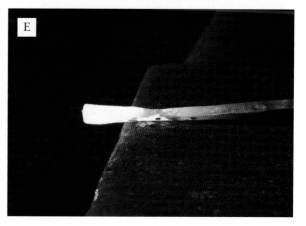

10. Squaring the bar

Forge the bar behind the taper to square it (A), then draw down the material to a centre point of the bar (B). Next, reverse taper out from the centre of the bar to the other end, creating a thinner bar section in the centre (C). Finally, form a 45-degree termination to mimic where a real rose would have been snipped from a bush (D & E).

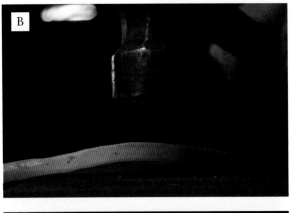

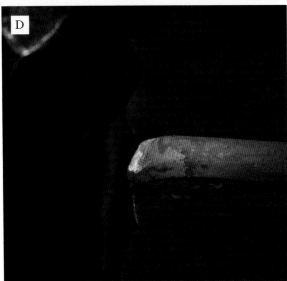

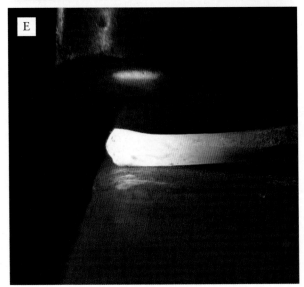

11. Forging the edges

Forge down the edges through square and octagonal to round, leaving a gently hammered texture on the stem (A). Once the forging is complete, rub the bar with a wire brush (B) and straighten the piece ready for the next step.

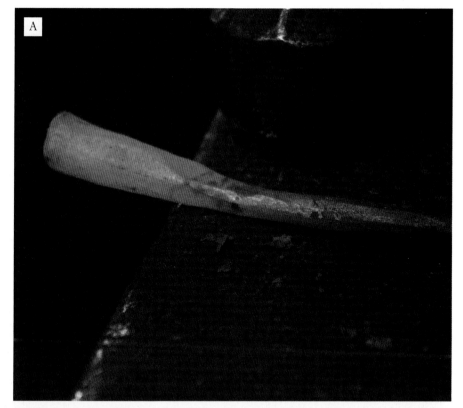

12. Creating sepals

Locking the stem in a vice with the upset end at the top (A), make a straight line to the centre of three sides, creating a triangle, as shown. Using either a hacksaw or an angle grinder, cut down in the lines 10–15mm (0.4–0.6in) deep (B). This will create three sepals – the leafy parts of a rose that support the flower head (C). Heat the material to orange temperature and then split the sepals apart using a hot chisel (D).

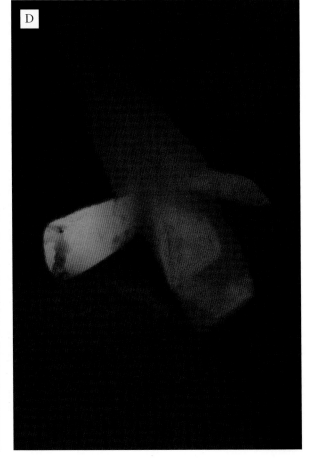

13. Bending the sepals

Using a metal face with a sharp corner, forge each of the newly cut and bent sepals into a taper (A), taking care to forge at an orange heat and to perform finishing blows at a cherry red or black heat (B). Once you've finished forging, scroll the sepals back in an organic way.

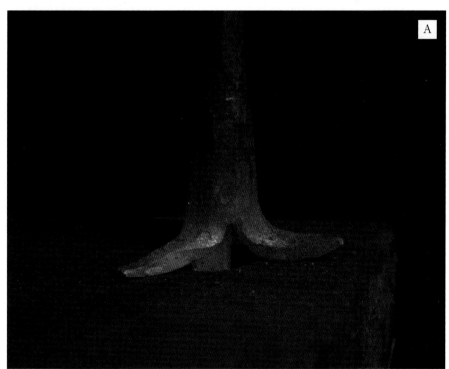

14. Forging a tenon
Now that the sepals have been created, forge what you can from the central piece of material to create a tenon (A). Finish the tenon by either filing or sanding on a belt grinder, until it is smooth (B).

15. Mounting the petals

Take each petal and centre punch the rough centre of each one (A). Drill the punched hole to the size of your tenon and fit to the stem (B & C), using a punch to push the petals down into place (D & E).

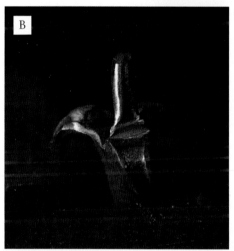

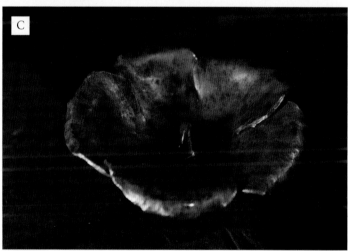

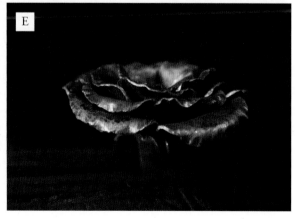

16. Riveting

Once everything is situated snugly, the stem and flower head can be riveted together. Use either a gas torch or the top of the fire to anneal the tenon if needed (A). The riveting can also be done cold, as the size allows for this. Using a punch and a hammer, rivet the tenon down until all parts of the flower are secure (B).

17. Fine fitting

To finish, heat the stem of the rose and shape and bend it to your liking. Wire brush the whole rose and apply beeswax to finish (see page 147).

MAKING FLAT BIT TONGS

Flat bit tongs are a practical and versatile tool, allowing you to hold various types of stock, including round or square bars as well as sheet metal. Tongs made with heavy stock take longer to heat up, allowing you to work on material for longer, and will also have a longer lifespan. However, heavy stock is more difficult to forge and creating tongs with it would be a fairly laborious task without the use of a power hammer. It is therefore a good idea to use lightweight stock for your first attempts.

Materials:
- 6mm (¼in) x 19mm (¾in) x 200mm (8in) mild steel bar
- 10 x 10mm (0.4 x 0.4in) round bar

Tools:
- Tongs, if cutting the bar down to size before forging (alternatively, use a bar with a 19mm (¾in) cut-out)
- French chalk/soapstone
- Centre punch and round punch
- Ball peen hammer
- Tongs
- Vice or a clamp on a metal bench
- Twisting tool
- Drift (3 per cent larger than rivet)
- Rivet (see page 196)

Skills and techniques used:
- Drawing out
- Rounding
- Planishing
- Setting down
- Punching

Key notes:
- Using a lighter-weight steel means that tongs can be quick and easy to make, allowing you to make many variations of the tool. You can create any tongs you find particularly useful out of a heavier stock at a later time.

The completed flat bit tongs.

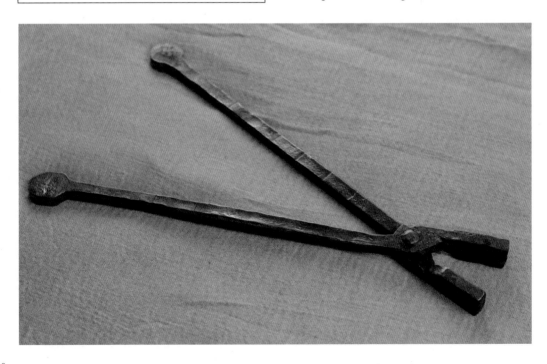

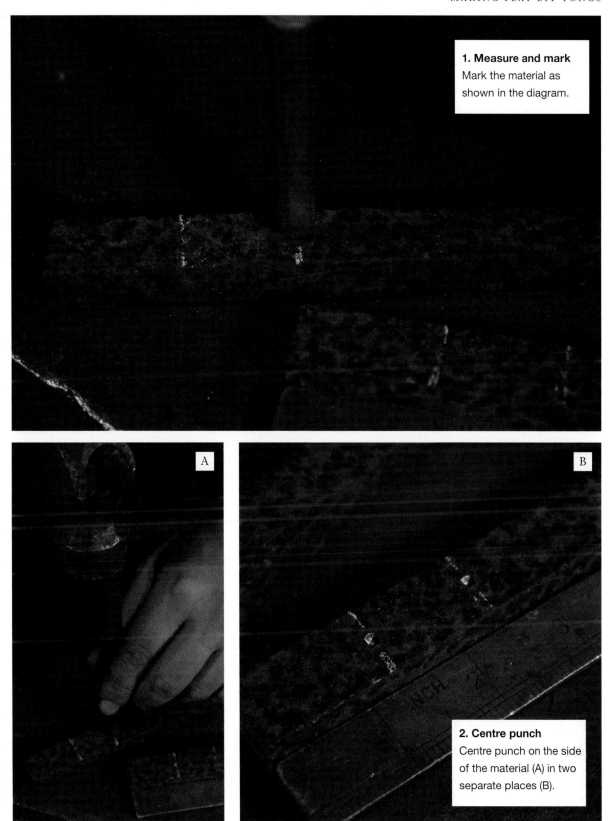

1. Measure and mark
Mark the material as shown in the diagram.

A

B

2. Centre punch
Centre punch on the side of the material (A) in two separate places (B).

3. Heating the bar

Heat the bar to orange temperature. The mark should still show up once the bar is heated (right).

4. Defining the hinge plate

The next step is to define the hinge plate. This is done by notching the bar in the previously marked areas. This process is similar to a set down, but without forging to a 90-degree angle. Start by holding the bar using tongs at an approximate angle of 45-degrees over the edge of the anvil on the first mark (below).

5. Forge the bar down

At a bright orange forging heat, forge the bar down to a third of its original width (A & B). Repeat this process for the second mark, remembering to flip the bar as shown (C & D).

6. Drawing out

Draw out the reins to the desired length, leaving a small amount of material at the end. Once drawn out to length, compare the two reins side by side (A) and adjust if needed, forging until both sides match in length (B–E).

7. Rounding the ends

At this point, the ends of the tongs can either be forged to a round- or straight-ended finish – which you do is down to personal preference.

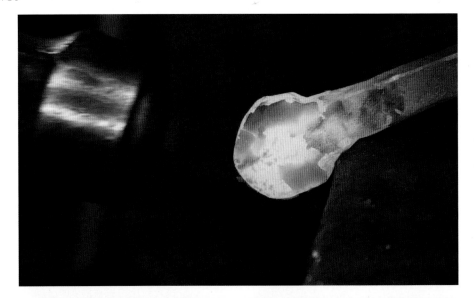

8. Chamfering the edges

Now that the reins are the same length, work can be done to make them safer to hold. You can do this by forging in the sharp square edges of the bar, giving it a chamfered edge (A, B & C). Then, finish by planishing at a low, cherry red heat (D) and removing any mishits. Make sure it is clamped at the junction between the jaws and the hinge plate.

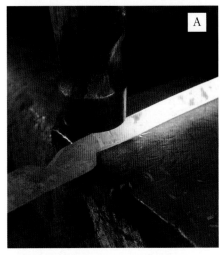

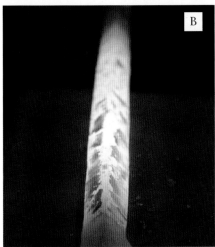

9. Forming the jaws

Form the jaws of the tongs. Heat the bar to a bright orange temperature, then clamp it in the vice and use a twisting tool to twist the jaw by 90 degrees (A). Repeat on the second tong blank, remembering to twist in the same direction as your first bend (B). Take some time to tidy up the corners of the transition between the jaws and the faceplate, using the edge of the anvil to ensure the transition is smooth and square (C & D).

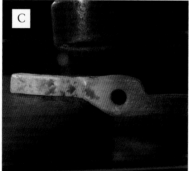

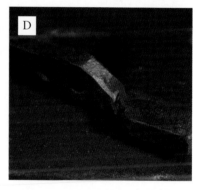

10. Punching the hole

Measure out the centre of the faceplate and centre punch a deep punch mark, allowing it to be easily found when heated. Bring the bar to a bright orange forging temperature and begin to punch through the faceplate until you have completely punched a hole. Don't forget to flip the bar over and place it over the anvil's pritchel hole to punch through the other side and push out the slug of material.

11. Widening the hole (right)

Using the punch, and keeping the material as close to forging temperature as possible, widen the hole you have created and use a drift to size the hole. The hole should be around 3 per cent bigger than your chosen rivet, as the steel will shrink by roughly this amount as it cools. Repeat this step for the other tong blank, punching the holes accurately to ensure the two sides later align.

12. Inserting the rivet (below)

Before heating the rivet, pack the coals tightly. This helps you to avoid losing the rivet in the fire, and also means you can keep an eye on it as it heats to ensure it doesn't burn. The rivet should measure the combined thickness of the faceplate, plus 1.5 times the diameter of the rivet. This rule can be applied to most cases when riveting is involved.

Once the rivet is up to a bright orange temperature, insert it through both of the faceplates of the tongs (A). Place the rivet head-down on the anvil and holding the reins of the tongs (B), hammer down on the top of the rivet, making sure you rotate the rings while doing so in order that you rivet evenly on all sides (C).

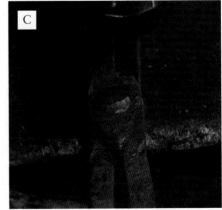

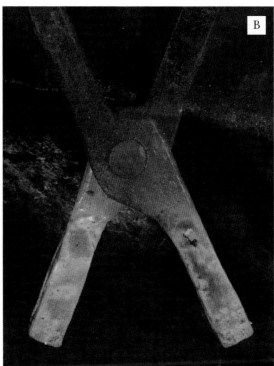

13. Loosening the tongs after riveting

After riveting, the tongs will be jammed in place (A). In order to loosen them and prepare them for use, heat the tong jaws to an orange temperature (B). You can then open and close them until you have a smooth, continuous range of motion.

Finally, quench the tool – you must continue opening and closing the tongs at this point to ensure they do not become stuck in place (C).

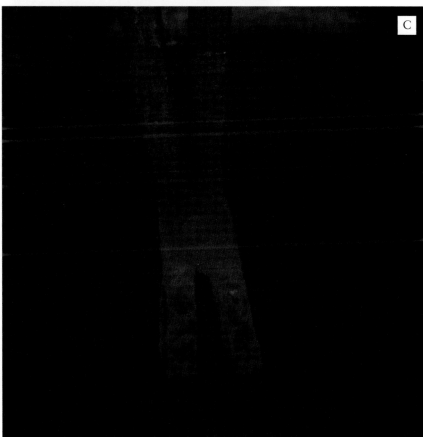

14. Creating the teeth

Heat to forging temperature the jaws of the tongs and insert a 10 x 10mm (0.4 x 0.4in) round bar as shown. Hammer down on the top of the tongs to create the teeth of the tong jaws (A).

Next, rotate the bar as shown (B), and repeat the hammering process to create a groove in the jaws (C). This will allow you to hold both round and square bars, making the tongs a versatile addition to your toolkit.

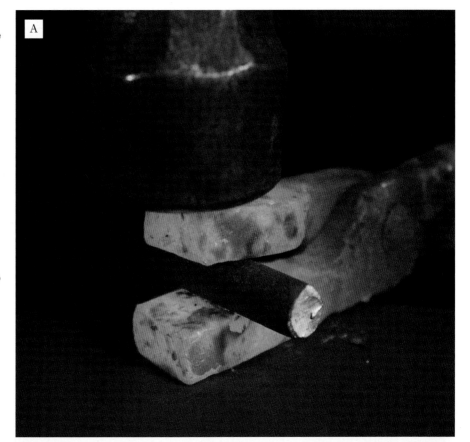

C

15. Setting the tongs

Set the tongs by heating up the jaws, hinge plate and the top of the reins and clamping the jaws on the stock you wish to hold (A), squeezing the reins together until they reach a comfortable holding position (B).

Making a forged knife

A general-purpose knife could be used for wood carving, bushcraft and other outdoor activities. The bevel – the ground angle and shape of the blade's edge – determines the sharpness, strength, durability and handling of a knife. The blade on this knife uses a Scandi (short for Scandinavian) grind. Also known as a zero grind, the Scandi grind contains a single bevel that runs to the edge at zero degrees, with no angle change along its length.

Part 1: The blade

Materials:
- 5 x 15cm (2 x 6in) flat steel bar

Tools:
- Forging hammer
- Flat bit tongs
- Ruler or set square and French chalk/soapstone
- Files/grinder (or belt grinder), or a hot cut tool
- Clamp
- Vegetable or canola oil and quenching container
- Magnet
- Oven

Skills and techniques used:
- Heat treatment hardening and tempering
- Precision grinding and knife sharpening

Key notes:
- As you are forging high carbon steel, the working temperature is a bright orange to dull yellow. If it's any lower, you can run the risk of cracking the material; any higher and you might decarbonize the steel.

- Forging a thin, flat bar tends to bend the bar into a U shape. This can be resolved by rotating the bar by 90 degrees and hitting the bar flat between steps.

The completed knife, with a steel blade and an antler and leather handle.

The material: 5 x 15cm (2 x 6in) flat steel bar.

1. Forging down the corners

Heat the bar to a bright orange (A). Using a forging hammer and holding the material in flat bit tongs, begin by forging down the corners of the bar at a 45-degree angle, to create the tip of the knife (B).

A

B

2. Avoiding defects

While forging the tip (A & B), you will notice that material starts to bunch up under the area that is being forged (C). If left alone, this material will form together and create what is known as a cold shut – a defect that can occur when metal folds over itself during forging. This can lead to cracks and lumps in the steel, compromising its integrity and resulting in potential breakage. To avoid this, lay the bar flat on the anvil face and hammer the bunched material flat between forging each side of the tip. Remember to reheat the steel once the bar cools to a red colour.

Once the tip has been formed, forge it down to one side of the bar, as shown (C), creating a curved knife point.

3. Forming the tip

Heat the whole length of the bar to a bright orange and hold it across the face of the anvil. Hammer down at a slight angle, gradually working towards the tip of the bar (which will become the tip of the knife's blade) to create a bevel (A). Flip the bar over, then work the material down across the bevel you have created (B). Continue to work both sides, aiming to keep the bevel quite short – as the steel used for this project is fairly thin, a shorter bevel will allow for a strong, sharp knife (C & D).

At a cherry red heat, very gently straighten out the bar (E), removing any twisting or unwanted curvature in the blade (F).

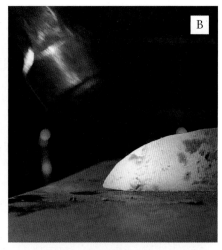

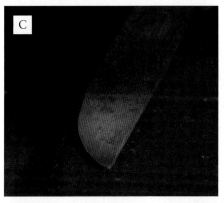

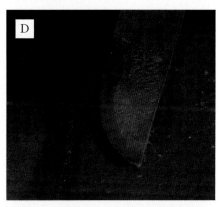

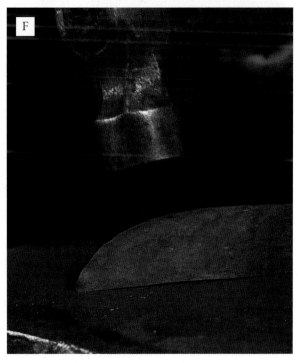

4. Marking out the tang

Measure from the tip of the blade down to 9cm (3½in) and mark it with chalk or soapstone (A). This marks the end of the blade and the start of the tang. The finished tang will have a 12mm (½in) width reduction from either side of the bar and be the same thickness as the rest of the knife. Mark these points (B–D).

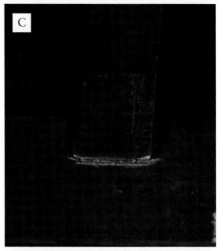

5. Hammering the edges

To forge the tang of the blade, heat the unworked end of the bar to an orange temperature, then create a set down, using the marks to help you.

6. Forging down the tang
Once the set down has been placed, forge down the tang, taking time to hammer down the edges and flat areas to keep the tang from becoming unnecessarily thick (A–D).

7. Refining the shoulders of the tang

The shoulders can be cut in by using a hot cut or by grinding them in, following the cutting marks you drew on (A–C). The cutting line should be perpendicular to the spine of the knife. If you've used a hot cut, the edges and corners must be filed smooth where the tang starts, to level it out and reduce the chance of stress fractures.

8. Normalizing

Before quenching can take place, three normalizing cycles (A & B) must be done to even the grain of the knife and remove any built-up stress from forging. Refer to the heat treatment chapter for more information. Always check the specifications of your steel and guidelines on heat treatment.

9. Filing the knife

Now that you have the general shape of your knife, the blade can be refined. Clamp the blade to the edge of a work surface and hand file it on the bevel (A & B), leaving a forged surface on the rest of the knife (C).

It should be noted that forge scale (also known as hammerscale) – the coating of oxide that forms on iron heated to forging temperatures – is harder than steel. This means that it will slow down, and possibly clog or dull, your file. It is therefore preferential to remove the scale layer with a belt grinder if possible before moving on to hand filing.

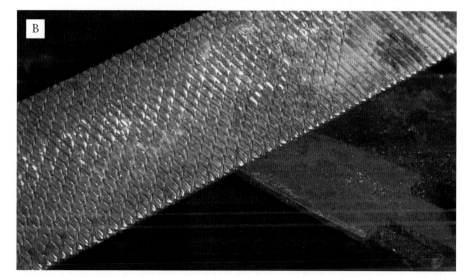

10. Bevelling the edge

File or grind the profile of the knife to the desired shape,
stopping once the edge of the bevel is at a thickness of
0.038mm (0.0015in). Next, profile and tidy up the tang
with the same filing or grinding method.

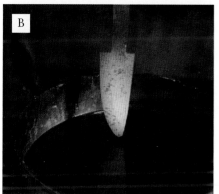

11. Heat treating

Now the blade should be heat treated. Warm the vegetable or canola oil until it is around the temperature of a warm bath and pour it into a fireproof quenching container. Heat the blade (A) and test its temperature with a magnet – once it is non-magnetic (which indicates that the steel has reached the Curie temperature, when it loses all magnetism), quench the blade in the pre-warmed oil (B–D). Run a file over the blade to test it – the file should skate over the surface of the steel rather than biting into it. When you're happy with this, place the knife into an oven preheated to 200°C/400°F/ gas mark 6 and leave it for two hours.

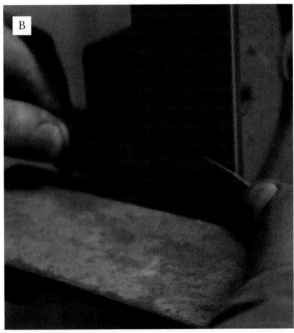

12. Belt grinder

Following heat treatment, filing is no longer a viable method of removing material; you'll need to sand the blade or use a whetstone if you do not have a belt grinder. If you are using a belt grinder, special care needs to be taken to avoid overheating the blade and ruining the heat treatment. Sand the blade (A–D), moving through progressively finer grits from 150 to 1,000. Throughout this process, ensure you have removed any scratches from the previous grit levels before moving on to a finer rating. At higher grits, a burr will show on one side of the blade – sharpen the other side to remove it, to leave a razor-sharp blade edge (opposite).

Part 2: The knife handle

The second part to this knife project is making a stacked leather handle. The full construction will use antler for the bolster and have a copper cap sandwiching a glued, stacked-leather handle. This handle is very durable and fairly weatherproof due to it having been soaked in linseed oil, making this knife a great all-rounder.

Materials:
- 35–45mm x 10mm (1.4-1.8in x 0.4in) antler
- 50 x 50mm (2 x 2in) square of 4mm (0.16in)-thick copper sheet
- 50 x 50mm (2 x 2in) squares of leather
- Tape
- Epoxy glue and ground charcoal
- Leather glue
- Linseed oil and steel wool

Tools:
- Steel ruler and a pen or pencil
- Leather punch or knife
- Hand drill or drill press
- Drill bit (of the thickness of the tang)
- Coping saw/jeweller's saw
- Vice and extra clamp
- Sharp knife
- Belt sander and hot cut tool

Key notes:
- Almost any fabric can be used for the stacking method with epoxy.

- Wood can be used instead of antler. The method of working is the same, including the need for a respirator to be worn while grinding or filing.

WARNING:
When working with bone, wear appropriate PPE. A respirator should be worn to avoid breathing in bone dust.

The completed knife blade and the marked-up antler.

1. Marking out

Using the tang of the knife, mark out the material to be removed from the antler, copper, and leather pieces (A). These markings should be made in the centre of the materials, as shown,

Once marked, use either a leather punch or a knife to cut the slits in the leather squares (B). For the antler and copper, drill the top and bottom marks with a drill bit that matches the thickness of the tang. The edge of the drill bit should be lined up with the marks on the antler and copper to ensure you do not remove too much material (C).

2. Saw blade

To remove the material left between the drill holes in the antler and copper, a coping or jeweller's saw can be used. Thread the saw blade through the hole and tension the saw carefully. Slowly applying light pressure, cut from one hole to the other, removing the material in-between. The channel can then be filed to fit snugly when put into place on the tang.

3. Taping the transition point

Before the knife is glued together it is important to tape the transition point between the knife blade and the handle to avoid getting epoxy on the finished blade.

4. Mixing and applying the epoxy

The epoxy can now be mixed. A small amount of ground charcoal has been added to darken the epoxy (A & B). Use the epoxy to fill any gaps in the fit-up between the bolster (antler) and the knife (C & D).

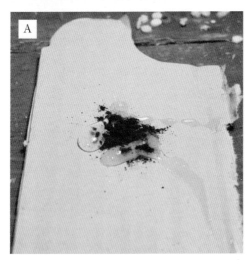

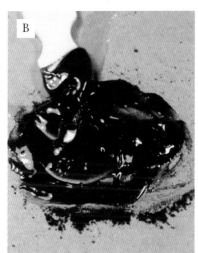

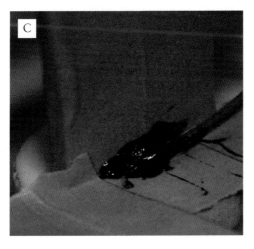

5. Stacking the leather

Once the bolster is in place, the leather squares can be stacked. Apply a layer of leather glue between each layer, and press down firmly when stacking.

6. Capping the handle

When around 10mm (0.4in) of the tang is left above the leather stack, fit the copper end cap on to the stack.

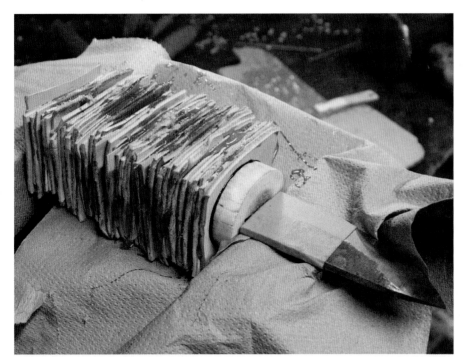

7. Clamping the stack
Place the stack in a vice with an extra clamp to apply even pressure. Leave the handle for the required amount of time for the glue to set (as detailed by the glue manufacturer).

8. Shaping the handle

To shape the stack, carefully use a sharp knife to carve
the leather away, removing the bulk of the material before
using a belt sander to finish, as the glue and leather will
bind and block the cutting surface of the belt.

9. Locking the handle into position
Using a hot cut, slice into the tang to lock the handle into place (warning: if the tang isn't annealed there is a risk of the knife breaking).

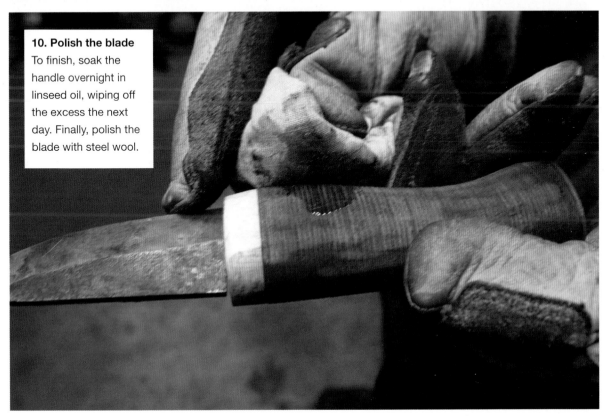

10. Polish the blade
To finish, soak the handle overnight in linseed oil, wiping off the excess the next day. Finally, polish the blade with steel wool.

Picture credits